D0282657

"A gorgeous reminder that walking is the most radical form of locomotion nowadays."

—**NICK OFFERMAN**, *Where the Deer and the Antelope Play: The Pastoral Observations of One Ignorant American Who Loves to Walk Outside*

"Inspired by Thoreau, but soon onto something that is very much his own, Ben Shattuck takes us on a journey that bores into the history of both himself and his native New England. A book of loss and redemption, fear and fragile hope, *Six Walks* is rich, evocative, and like the boat gunwale that cuts off the tip of his finger, unexpectedly dangerous—in that best of Thoreauvian ways."

—**NATHANIEL PHILBRICK**, *Travels with George: In Search of Washington and His Legacy*

"I think Thoreau would have liked this book, and that's a high recommendation."

—**BILL McKIBBEN**, *The End of Nature*

"By walking in Thoreau's footsteps, Ben Shattuck ends up following the long trail left by wandering thinkers and writers like Rousseau, Muir, Walser, Benjamin, and Solnit. Along the way, *Six Walks* offers a moving meditation on nature and history—and what our precarious place between these two realms may be."

—**HERNAN DIAZ**, *In the Distance*

"Walking as means of healing, walking as a way of seeing what's there, walking as a method of pulling you out of yourself and rejoining the world—in this beautiful, smart, and moving book, Ben Shattuck shows us where putting one foot in front of the other can take us. Thoreau's footsteps serve as map, but Shattuck has made a fresh journey right into the heart of things. In painterly prose, he brings us along on his walks and proves the best sort of guide: curious, open to the chance encounter, deeply attuned to rhythms natural and personal and to the strange joys to be found even in periods of pain. Most of all, he reminds us, every step of the way, of what's on offer every time we walk out the door."

—**NINA MacLAUGHLIN**, *Summer Solstice: An Essay*

"A beautiful and thought-provoking journey of discovery, which will leave you very glad that you walked a while with Ben Shattuck."

—**ERIC JAY DOLIN**, *A Furious Sky: The Five-Hundred-Year History of America's Hurricanes*

SIX WALKS

Copyright © 2022 by Ben Shattuck

All rights reserved. No part of this book may be used or reproduced in any manner whatsoever without written permission from the publisher except in the case of brief quotations embodied in critical articles or reviews. For information, contact Tin House, 2617 NW Thurman St., Portland, OR 97210.

Published by Tin House, Portland, Oregon

Distributed by W. W. Norton & Company

Library of Congress Cataloging-in-Publication Data
Names: Shattuck, Ben, 1984- author.
Title: Six walks : in the footsteps of Henry David Thoreau / Ben Shattuck.
Description: Portland, Oregon : Tin House, [2022] | Includes bibliographical references.
Identifiers: LCCN 2021050923 | ISBN 9781953534040 (hardcover) | ISBN 9781953534095 (ebook)
Subjects: LCSH: New England—Description and travel. | Walking—New England. | Shattuck, Ben, 1984-—Travel—New England.
Classification: LCC F10 .S53 2022 | DDC 974—dc23/eng/20211206
LC record available at https://lccn.loc.gov/2021050923

First US Edition 2022
Printed in the USA
Interior design by Jakob Vala

www.tinhouse.com

"Cape Cod," "Interlude I," "Mount Katahdin," "Interlude II," "Wachusett Mountain," "Home": An earlier version of these sections appeared in *The Common* under the title "Three Walks." www.thecommononline.org/three-walks

"When I went farther up . . ." on page 101: From *Little Weird*s by Jenny Slate, copyright © 2019. Reprinted by permission of Little, Brown and Company, an imprint of Hachette Book Group, Inc.

"Interlude III": An earlier version of this section appeared in The Paris Review Daily under the title "Farewell to Winter, Farewell to My Fingertip." www.theparisreview.org/blog/2018/03/26/farewell-to-winter-farewell-to -my-fingertip

SIX WALKS

In the Footsteps of
Henry David Thoreau

BEN SHATTUCK

TIN HOUSE / Portland, Oregon

footstep |ˈfŏŏt̯ˌstep|

A step taken by a person in walking, especially as heard by another person.

Part One

We will remember within what walls we lie, and understand that this level life too has its summit, and why from the mountain-top the deepest valleys have a tinge of blue; that there is elevation in every hour, as no part of the earth is so low that the heavens may not be seen from, and we have only to stand on the summit of our hour to command an uninterrupted horizon.

—Henry David Thoreau, twenty-five years old
(July 1842)

Cape Cod

The idea to follow Henry David Thoreau's walks came while I was standing in the shower at dawn one May morning, listening to the water drill my skull and lap my ears, wondering what I could do to stop the dreams of my past girlfriend. This was years ago, in my early thirties, when I couldn't find a way out of the doubt, fear, shame, and sadness that had arranged a constellation of grief around me. In this last dream, the one that got me into the shower at sunrise, she was in labor. I dreamt that she had a husband—dark-haired, wearing a red shirt with sleeves rolled to his elbows—who stood bed-side, gripping her hand while she breathed. I stood against the wall, touching a white handkerchief that I wanted to offer them. She looked up at her husband. He closed his hands over hers. I wanted to leave the room, but stayed because my legs weren't working just then. I kept touching the hem of the handkerchief. The baby came. There were three of us in the room, and then there were four.

In the shower, between the scenes of the birth, came to me images of a young, bearded man standing on an empty beach, wind whipping at his coattails, the ocean pounding in front of him. He was smiling. Plainly happy. I saw him crouch to pick up a bone of driftwood. I saw him in a lighthouse, writing in his journal by a flickering candle flame; wading through dune grass—walking stick clocking with each step. It was Henry, pictured from his book *Cape Cod*, which I'd been reading every night that week.

I stepped from the shower. Out the window, the tide, set higher than usual by some phase of the moon, drowned the marsh grass. The blush of sunrise candied the water pink. Living by a salt marsh on the southern coast of Massachusetts, I noticed the passing of a day divided by the floor of the landscape dropping and rising. High tides feel favorable, as does anything overfull—waterfall, blooming peony, snowbent tree limb, spilt milkweed seeds. The high tide felt purposeful, then. The ocean leaning inland, urging.

I dressed quickly in my bathing suit and a sweater, made a cup of coffee, emptied my backpack onto the kitchen table and filled it with a loaf of bread, a brick of cheddar cheese, three apples, a bag of carrots, a rain jacket, and my copy of *Cape Cod*.

I was—I knew then—going to Cape Cod. I would walk the outer beaches, from the elbow to Province-town's fingertip, as Henry had done. If it took a day, or three, I didn't mind. I had nothing else to do that week. Days before, I'd driven all the way to a mon-astery in Vermont to choose ceramics for an exhibit I was curating about art made by monks and nuns, and on the way back stopped by my old high school for the reception of a recent painting show—a show on which I'd worked too hard and included too many paintings, because, probably, of adolescence's anxious cinders still warm in me, decades later. I didn't feel like painting anything, anymore, for a long time.

Before I walked out the door that morning, I also put a notebook in my backpack, not because I ever journaled or made sketches, but because Henry had, and I wanted to try someone else's habits for a few days.

During the hour drive from my home to the Cape, I fantasized that I'd replicate the peace and higher per-spective Henry had documented in that seam of land

and sea. "The sea-shore is a sort of neutral ground," he wrote, "a most advantageous point from which to contemplate this world." I didn't expect sublime perspective; I hoped only for a respite from my nightmares, for the waves and wind and weather to reshape the masses of my subconscious as they had shifted the dunes of Wellfleet, Truro, and Provincetown. Isn't this always the hope, heading out for a long walk? That in your aloneness the landscape will relieve you? That your mind will be renewed, calmed?

I crossed the Bourne Bridge and sped into a roundabout, driving so fast that my coffee mug tumbled from the cup holder.

When Henry started this walk at age thirty-two in 1849, he wore a broad-brimmed hat designed with a miniature shelf to hold the flowers he found. He dressed in an earthen-toned three-piece suit, and always carried his spyglass for bird-watching. His knapsack was rigged with a compartment for his books—one for pressing flowers—his sewing materials, his fishing line, and a handful of fishing hooks. He walked with an umbrella tilted over his shoulder to keep the sand and wind off his neck, and with a special walking stick doubling as a ruler that he used to measure plants. He took a goose-quill pen with which he wrote in luxurious horizontal flourishes—his *y*'s look windblown, the crosses of his *t*'s like distant hills. He packed salt for seasoning, sugar and tea, and a "junk of heavy cake" with plums. He was a sinewy, exercised country saunterer, handsomely dressed and carrying with him all the items for misadventure, like a flowery battleship.

Whereas I, standing on the Nauset dunes and staring out to the open palm of the Atlantic, looked as if I'd just disembarked a red-eye and had a deep misunderstanding of the current season. The cold May morning wind seized my legs, exposed beneath my bathing suit, but I was sweating from the waist up under two shirts, a sweater, a rain jacket, and a winter hat. Henry wore special boots that he slathered with paraffin; my running shoes were held together in the front with duct tape. The sand tore away this tape in the first mile before filleting the soles of the shoes halfway off, so I tied the shoes to my backpack, which meant that in the next couple of days, the dozens of miles of sand would knead blisters between my toes, on the uppermost part of the arch, and, weirdly, on the very tops of my big toes. But the worst was the sun. I hadn't packed any sunscreen. And because summer in New England comes like a gunshot after winter, my calves would go from ice white to red by the time I stumbled up to a stranger's house in Wellfleet many hours later, knocking on the door and hoping for a place to sleep, because, as it turned out, I'd also forgotten a sleeping bag in my rush to escape my own bed.

The beach is "a vast morgue," Henry wrote, "where famished dogs may range in packs, and crows come daily to glean the pittance which the tide leaves them."

You usually come to the seashore to spend the day with broad wings of sand flanking your sides and the fan of ocean in front—you plant an umbrella and dash into the water a few times. Beaches aren't known or loved for hiking, because, I soon realized, they offer a monotonous, unchanging landscape. On my left, for miles, a hundred feet of red sand and clay peeking into a salt-killed rim of bayberry, huckleberry, and the odd scrub pine wherein song sparrows trilled the famous first notes of Beethoven's Fifth. To my right, the flat sea, profound at first but unremarkable thereafter. And so my eyes fell to the ground, to this "vast morgue," to see what items the ocean had returned to shore that morning. Beaches do have a tang of fate. The smooth stones, the ringed stones, the tired driftwood, the dead loon—crook-necked and constellated in white dots on

ALL ILLUSTRATIONS BY BEN SHATTUCK

WOODEN CHAIR ON THE OUTER BEACH

black feathers—seem there for a reason. The Legos, cow femur, wooden chair propped upright and facing out to sea, three pennies whose Lincolns had worn to blurry portraits, nickel reduced to the size and thinness of a dime, Red Sox hat, Patriots hat, fish vertebrae, and giant bullet shell whose tip had filigreed to metal lacework.

I walked for over an hour before I saw another person: a bird-watcher, with his telescope set up in the middle of the beach. We talked dead loons, northern gannets, and which shorebirds were migrating. Even with the long pauses of strangers meeting, I was happy for the distraction, as it momentarily halted the conveyor belt of sadness that the dream was still moving through me. I'd rather dream of the bizarre ships sent from my subconscious, the ones floating on waves of anxiety and fear—dreams of two-headed snakes, of my teeth going soft, of my house filled with small, sharp-toothed rodents. I'd rather the puzzles, images to be interpreted, distanced by a measure of analysis and rephrased for the day. What I'd gotten the previous night was different: a real person, put in material textures of everyday life. More like experience. Memory. Not a puzzle floating on anything—just a cold dunk in the sea itself. That's why I was clinging, now, to the birder, thrashing at him with questions about the migratory routes of loons.

The bird-watcher, clearly wanting to end the conversation, wished me well, folded up his telescope, and left to find some shorebird he was searching for.

I sat in the sand and, to distract myself, took out my journal and wrote synonyms for the wind: *cloud-river, weather's yeast, season trader, colonial fuel.* It was a word game I'd assigned freshman college students one day years earlier, when I'd finished teaching the lesson plan but still had fifteen minutes before the end of the period. "Look out the window," I'd said, "and write the longest list of synonyms you can for anything out there." Sitting at my desk ten minutes later, listening to the students read their lists aloud, I was unexpectedly moved—entranced, maybe. This renaming of nature, these many words for an oak tree or the clouds or the sky or the Iowa River, sounded like prayers, like worship. I think everyone in the classroom felt it, because we all entered the silence you feel in a church or theater. The spell was broken when a boy started his list with "Worm shit."

"Dirt?" I said.

"The earth."

Hurricane muscle, summer's respite, crying scapegoat.

FISH VERTEBRA

My only goal that first day on Cape Cod was to find the house where Henry slept, which was near a pond in Wellfleet, ten miles from my starting point, and to ask whoever was inside to take my picture beside it. Then I'd go off to sleep in the woods or on the beach. I preferred an uncomfortable bed in those days, because it could smother nightmares. If I woke from a nightmare, I sometimes took my blanket to the living room couch or down to the floor beside the bed.

It's in Wellfleet where Henry, knocking on doors to find lodging, meets an eighty-eight-year-old oysterman who brags that when he was a teenager during the American Revolution, he heard cannon fire echoing across Massachusetts Bay, from Concord. And now, in the mid-1800s, the oysterman says, "I am a poor, good-for-nothing crittur . . . I am all broken down this year." He lets Henry stay the night.

I couldn't find the oysterman's house, because I couldn't match any of the vistas in *Cape Cod*. The plains that Henry saw when he was there have been drowned by forests of evergreens, home to seemingly a thousand wild turkeys. Walking through the pines around Wellfleet's seven outer ponds, my footfalls silenced by carpets of ochre and shed needles, I quickly got lost.

In the late afternoon, I sat down at one pond's edge to watch alewives nibble at the surface of clear water. I was wondering how cold it would get that night, hoping I'd manage without a sleeping bag, when a couple appeared on a dirt road circling the pond. The man was walking with a bad knee, and the woman—his daughter, maybe—walked patiently beside him.

I took the cheddar block from my backpack, cut cubes, and ate them from the side of my knife. I flicked cheese shavings to the alewives, which darted to the surface. Listening to the wind shushing through the pines, watching the fish swim under a glaze of moving clouds, I imagined my experience wasn't far from Henry's. What a poetically cruel compound, *alewives*.

When the couple reached me, I wrapped up the cheese block, stood, smiled, waved.

"Are you local?" I asked.

They said they were, and so I asked if they knew where Henry David Thoreau had stayed when he was here. "Back in 1849," I said.

They didn't know.

"Maybe you could point me to any old houses in the area?" I asked.

The woman pointed me down a road, said there was an older house that way.

I thanked them, then continued, quickly getting lost again, and found myself walking toward a grassy clearing in which stood a colonial era Cape Cod–style home. A woman, knee-deep in a flower garden—tulips, daffodils—watched me. Beside her were orange halves, stuck faceup on a bird feeder to welcome Baltimore orioles, something my mom also did in the spring.

"Hello!" I called.

She smiled. Waved.

"I'm looking for the house where Thoreau stayed," I said.

"Oh, yes," she called. "It's just right there." She pointed her trowel across the pond.

I introduced myself.

"I'm Pat," she said.

Just then, a man with a pair of oars balanced over his shoulder emerged from behind a nearby shed.

"I'm going fishing," he said to Pat. He looked at me, confused.

"This young man is looking for the Thoreau house," Pat said to him. "That's my husband, Randy," she said to me.

"Right there," he said, nodding toward the pond. "I can row you, if you want."

Minutes later, Randy and I were out on the water, in a fishing dory he described as "a boat made by people in Vermont who don't know how to make boats." We cut through the pond by their house, through a channel and into another pond, over shoots of young lily pads still underwater and reaching for the surface. Schools of alewives scattered at the bow. The only sounds were the slow creak of his oars sighing on the oarlocks and the slush of water on wood. He landed the dory ashore, below the house, and told me to take my time—he'd be fishing.

"Holler when you want to be picked up," he said, and then slid away from the shore.

I peered at the house. Through the windows I could see low ceilings, low doors. Beautiful in the way most anything wooden and built before the Industrial Revolution is. Placed well on the land, with its many boxy pieces atop a granite foundation. But I felt no connection, no insight, no sudden power.

Years earlier, I'd been a Civil War reenactor, and had gotten to think quite a lot about inhabiting the past— about when the past is easy to access and feel, and when it's hard. Camping on the manicured lawns between the monuments at Gettysburg doesn't give you a sensation of the past, but marching on a rarely visited battlefield in Virginia, for instance, in which the land looks like it did in the 1860s, does. I felt actual fear when I stared at a line of a couple thousand Confederate reenactors. When the cannons fire, you flinch, then see the smoke clouds drift across the field, and eventually you smell gunpowder. It was only then, facing the other side, that I felt how cruel and absurd the process had been for strangers to line up and murder each other. I looked at portraits of Civil War soldiers after my summer of reenacting and felt only angry: at the Southern politicians who enacted secession, who defended slavery and then let people squat on a field to be shot at. The past is a verb, I found that summer. Its feeling comes through participation, not standing in front of a monument.

I looked at the house, then at the pond. I saw Randy cast his line and slowly reel it in. I sat on the lawn, took a couple of notes, then ambled down to the pond's edge and motioned toward him. He stowed the rod, then eased his oars back into the water.

"Did you find what you were looking for?" he said when the dory's bow touched the mucky rim.

I shrugged, said I thought so.

"Where were you going to sleep tonight?" he asked as he rowed us away.

"Maybe on the beach?"

"On the beach? You'll freeze. It's going to get down to forty. You can stay with us."

The sky had turned brittle and cold with the clouds closing out the blue. I thanked him, said I could pay for the night.

"Don't worry about it," he said.

"Thanks," I said. I felt my anxiety loosen and float away.

Some time ago, I wrote an essay about napping outside—how I would, for instance, see a carpet of moss in the forest or a cradle of rocks on a summit, and then feel inexplicably tired, lie down, and fall asleep quicker than I ever could in a bed. How, also, I'd awoken in a blizzard on a mountainside; another time in a graveyard with two men standing over me, asking if I was "practicing"; woke in a field with a mouse in my pocket eating the peanuts I carried. I felt a freedom to be in the wilderness that I know is not given to everyone. I was safe in a way that is unequally bestowed, and this was again obvious during that first walk and those that came after. The fact that I didn't care where I slept those nights—or that I wasn't required to care where I slept—likely had little to do with how polite or ingratiating I could be. Free movement through spaces—in a

THE OYSTERMAN'S HOUSE; WELLFLEET

forest, along a beach, among a community—depended on the fact that I'd likely not be seen as threatening—as white—and likely not be threatened—as a man. Whom I got to talk to, and why they talked to me, depended on having this body.

I thought of Henry's displeasure with his own body, which he wrote about in moments throughout his journals, and yet how it was the legally and culturally privileged body at the time, the free and voting body during slavery and a generation before women's suffrage. "I must confess there is nothing so strange to me as my own body," he wrote in his journal the winter of 1842. "I love any other piece of nature, almost, better." But his body would not be violated without the consequence of law; it would be protected by its particular stretch of skin and hormones and organs.

I was a white man in a linen shirt and wool socks. In my personal experience, in this part of the country, no one had ever called the police because I was in their yard or knocking on their door.

Randy rowed us around the pond casually, pointing to where it had changed over the course of his life.

When we landed back at the house, by way of thanks, I dug three holes and planted three big rosebushes that were waiting in pots beneath their windows.

"The winds howled around the house," Henry wrote of his overnight at the oysterman's, just across the pond from where I was staying. The wind made the "fire-boards as well as the casements rattle well that night."

I heard no wind, lying in an antique bed. My legs were still burning from the day's sun, and I felt my heart-beat in my feet, but I was warm and brightly happy in a way that comes with unexpected luck. Without a plan, with only an impulse to walk, I'd finished the day here: in the home of kind strangers who'd served fried scal-lops for dinner and told stories about winter ice fishing on the pond just out their door. I had a clear feeling that I was supposed to end up here.

"The kids and I would skate around the pond, set-ting fishing lines," Pat had said as we ate. "And then come back into the house to watch with binoculars, see if the lines moved. We rolled dice to pick who was the unlucky one to go back out and reel in the fish." There are families like theirs still, huddled in a seaside house in the middle of winter, in our century, deciding who will skate out for dinner. A family in Henry's time probably spent a day like this, playing games and ice fishing, too. It comforted me to think that technology hadn't taken away the satisfaction of a warm house on a winter day. Fish can still be caught, fires lit. No matter how crowded our lives feel, the old ways haven't entirely disappeared. You can still reach back for some of them.

I was too tired to dream that night, and so was spared a small measure of humiliation, the feeling that during my days I carried inside an anxious and sad person who surfaced when I slept. "I don't dream anymore," I told a friend that year. "More like my subconscious just pile-driving me in sleep."

I was sad to walk away from Wellfleet the next morning, with the sun filtering through the pines, illuminating the garden and the new orange halves Pat had arranged for the orioles. I sat outside with coffee, watching the birds first arrive in the surrounding canopies, then cautiously drop down to the oranges and sink their beaks into the pulp. For breakfast, back in 1849, Henry ate eels, green beans, doughnuts, and tea. I had cinnamon toast and cheesy eggs, then left, promising to write Randy and Pat when and if I got to Provincetown, still twenty miles or so to the north.

The cliffs near Truro are composed of terra-cotta-red clay, which had trickled down to the beach in chunks, leaving rusty lines in the pale sand. I picked up a wedge as big as a slice of wedding cake, smelled it, and had the sudden urge to bite it. The chunk dissolved, milk-chocolate-like, when I massaged it with my tongue into the roof of my mouth.

Is it possible to go to a beach today and not consider climate change? I thought, while trying to suck out bits of Cape Cod that had gotten stuck between my teeth. The Cape's arm withers west every year, shedding its sand and clay, accelerated by climate change. At the same time, pausing to consider the shifting blues furling out under the morning sun, I wondered if people will ever stop loving the sea— this weapon we've created out of climate change. As in, when it finally rolls in, will there be a few of us staring out to the horizon still, admiring the vast beauty that just ruined us? Rising global temperatures recently placed Henry's journals into popular view: a few Massachusetts biologists used his records of wildflowers' nineteenth-century bloom dates to compare to present-day bloom dates. Flowers were not opening on schedule, they saw, which divided the flowers from their pollinators' schedules. Highbush blueberry, for one, was flowering in eastern Massachusetts a full three weeks earlier than it did in the nineteenth century.

WHERE HE SLEPT — TRURO LIGHT

"At length," Henry wrote once, "as we plodded along the dusty roads, our thoughts became as dusty as they; all thought indeed stopped, thinking broke down, or proceeded only passively in a sort of rhythmical cadence of the confused material of thought." By midmorning, walking had smoothed my mind some, snipped away rattling worry.

I opened my notebook, writing that I'd found the house where Henry stayed, but that I'd felt no transcendent experience. I did love the windows, though. I noted the baritone rumble of waves presently dropping themselves on the beach, the gulls pinwheeling overhead. There, to the south, was a charcoal cloudbank, and the sound of thunder carried on the wind. A whale's mouth broke the water then, a sight that landed in my brain where fire does—shaking out ordered thought. The black wedge—the mouth—dwarfed a seagull nearby. The whale sped forward, turned, sped back. The tail rose. The whale could have been fifty feet long, I saw then, as the gull took a few wingbeats to make it from mouth to tail. Around the same time, I later read, on the other side of the Atlantic, a sperm whale washed up on Spanish coast with an entire greenhouse inside it: plastic tarps, hoses, ropes, flowerpots, and a spray canister.

I found an apple in my pack, divided it into quarters, and watched the whale plow the sea.

Shellacked in rain, like rubies nestled in enormous sienna carpets, wild cranberries appeared in the boggy ground between the hills outside Provincetown. I'd made it in two days. *The rain sounds like oil sizzling in a pan*, I wrote in my journal. I untied the shoes from my backpack, slipped them onto my blistered feet.

Evening had settled in by the time I walked onto the town's streets.

I ducked into the first pub I saw, sliding my walking stick—a piece of driftwood that I still have—into an umbrella stand. The pub was low-ceilinged, candlelit, crowded with people fogging up the windows. There was one seat left at the bar, beside an elderly woman wreathed in a zebra-print scarf, with a bob of frizzy blond hair and thick-rimmed glasses.

"What do you put on the table?" she said, scowling, when I sat down. She clutched her cocktail glass.

"What do I put on the table?"

"You heard me," she said. She slapped the bar.

She was alone. Her lipstick was printed over the rim of her glass. I wondered if she'd been saving this seat for someone, or if this was the night she'd designed for herself.

"I guess I put it all on the table," I said, because if I've learned anything from novels, it's that you talk with a stranger at a bar when they talk to you.

"Did you hear that?" she said to the bartender, who smiled politely and slipped me a menu. She laughed, and coughed the rattling cough of a long-time smoker.

"Good answer," she said. "I'm Dora." She held out her hand, tipped with long, red fingernails. I introduced myself.

She didn't ask why I was wearing a wet bathing suit, or where I had come from. Instead, she demanded I guess her age. I guessed lower than her seventy-one, and she waved at the bartender. "He said sixty!"

"Good guess," the bartender said to me, smirking.

I ordered shrimp, which was one of the very few times I'd speak while I was sitting at the bar. Without my asking, she then explained without pause that she owned five restaurants, that money was important for a happy life, that she had been good friends with Providence's mayor-turned-felon Buddy Cianci and he'd come into her restaurants, that she'd been coming to Provincetown since the seventies and everyone here (at this, she swept her hand over her head to gesture around the room) knew her, that she loved New York City, and that last spring she'd had just a really nice day buying neckties with the disgraced TV personality Matt Lauer.

She became quiet, took a gulp of her drink, and asked for another vodka.

"You're probably too young to have any regrets," she said.

I didn't feel like explaining that I was on a walk to escape nightmares about a breakup, so I asked if she had regrets.

"I wouldn't marry my first husband," she said. "And I wouldn't marry my second husband. Maybe not my third. They all cheated. Cheated, cheated, cheated. My first husband, he was a long-distance swimmer. He used to swim out in the sea. Way, way out. I'd sit on the beach, watch him, hope he wouldn't come back. You know there are sharks out here?"

The bartender put a plate of shrimp in front of me. I ate while Dora talked about men, about there being good ones and bad ones, and how they were just born that way and there was nothing you could do about it.

She suddenly said we should go, asked for the bill, and told the bartender to include my dinner.

"No, it's okay," I said, partly because I didn't want her to pay, but mostly because I was still hungry from the walk and had finished only half the plate.

"Oh, quiet," she said, waving her hand in my face. "Just be a gentleman and walk me home."

The bartender put down the bill, which came to sixty-four dollars. Dora set out her credit card, and then left a one-hundred-dollar tip.

"Ready?" she said.

She slipped off the stool, grabbed my shoulder to steady herself. I saw then how small she was. Five feet, maybe less.

"Let's go!" she said.

Her scarf fell to the ground as she swerved toward the exit.

I was exhausted and hungry, but watching her tilt into a passing waiter, I didn't see how I could stay. I ate one more bite of shrimp, then waved at the bartender, who mouthed, *Good luck*. I left my walking stick in the umbrella rack, and pushed through the door.

I found her outside, swaying beside a puddle.

A warm, humid night had settled in behind the passing rain.

"Did you walk?" I asked.

"Did you?" she replied. I nodded.

"Then we'll walk," she said.

She hooked her arm around my elbow, and we crossed the street. I wondered how far I'd need to take her. I wanted to get out of my wet clothes, to find a motel where I could finish writing down my notes from the day. Above us, the trees dripped rain into the puddles along the sidewalk. When a gust of wind came, rain shook from the leaves and fell on us. She stopped, turned to me.

"We've met before," she said. "Who are you?"

I told her my name again. "We haven't met before," I said.

"That's not what I meant," she said. She leaned in, lowering her voice to a hoarse whisper. She touched my shoulder, then stood right in front of me, toe-to-toe. Her head, down by my chest, tilted up, as if she were about to kiss me.

"I mean, where did you come from?" she asked. She pushed her glasses up to the top of her blond frizz.

I smiled, told her I was on a walk.

She shook her head. "That's not what I meant," she said, sadly.

"Where do you live?" I asked, stepping back.

She turned around. "There." She pointed to the house directly beside the bar.

We walked back across the street.

"I have an extra bed," she said, standing at the door. "You can stay if you want."

"Okay," I said.

"Come in, then," she said.

Just then the door swung open and a man filled it.

"You're back," his voice boomed.

"Quiet," she said to him. "This is my new husband." She tugged on my arm. "He's staying with us tonight."

"Excuse me?" the man said. He was angry. He was tall, broad, and looked younger than Dora by a decade. I felt immediately scared.

He looked at me. He noted, I'm sure, my appearance in a way that Dora had not: the torn duct tape on my shoes, the bathing suit, the raincoat, my beard.

"Come in," he said to Dora, putting his arm over her shoulder and starting to close the door.

She batted him away.

"My new husband is staying with us tonight as my guest."

He smiled, sighed, turned to me.

"No, that's fine," I said, also smiling.

"No!" she said, grabbing my wrist. "I offered you a bed in my home, and you are staying here."

The man then said to me, "It's very nice of you to drop her off. I'm sorry she's made you do that. We don't have any rooms for you to sleep in. Good night."

He yanked her hand from my wrist and pulled her inside, and as he shut the door, she yelled my name. Yelled it as if I was far away.

I went back for my walking stick, and then continued into town. I wouldn't be able to sleep now, shaken by the man, by Dora's drunkenness, by the image of her watching her ex-husband swim in the distance and hoping that he would drown or be taken under—that all her problems would be taken away by a shark. How it was somehow easier to sit on a beach, hoping for something as impossibly rare as an animal attack, rather than leave him. How she wanted an ancient predator to save her, to punish him for his infidelity. How she made a small god out of the shark, and prayed for it at the edge of the sea. And how the gods never really do come in that way.

The streetlights reflected in the puddles as I walked.

Downtown, music thumped from a bar's open door. I shuffled toward it. A man at the door waved me in. I hid my walking stick and, with my backpack still on, moved through a dark hallway, toward the music, right onto the dance floor, into a swaying

PROVINCETOWN, NIGHT

crowd. Over my head, lasers pulsed in a cloudbank made by fog machines. Red. Blue. Green. The ceiling was black, outer space overhead. Something like the sound of a tornado warning overtook the music, followed by halting then tattooing drums. Bodies pressed against each other, spreading warmth. It felt as though I'd left the Wellfleet ponds weeks ago, though it had been just that morning.

I'm not sure Henry would have liked all the noise in Provincetown. The cars, the crowds, the music in the streets—this was a man who wrote the line "Why was there never a poem on the cricket?" But surrounded by the music and all the swaying bodies, I wondered if there was some part of him that would have liked to have been out on the dance floor, fluttering his hands up and into the red lasers. Happy to have ended his journey at one big party.

That night I knocked on the doors of five B&Bs. The first three were filled. The fourth one was also filled, I assumed, because someone inside just waved at me through the window to go away. I slept that night in a B&B that would have been called a boarding-house at one time: in a room without a bathroom that could be covered crosswise in three steps and lengthwise in five. With its one window, one chair, and bedside table, it reminded me of the famous van Gogh room in the Saint-Rémy asylum.

I draped my damp clothes on the chair and the table, and was cold most of the night because the heat wasn't on and I couldn't find a thermostat. I wished I'd brought a change of clothes, or that Dora's fourth husband had been more like her—either happily drunk or blindly trusting.

The next morning, at a café in downtown Provincetown, an artist named Mary pushed the *New York Times* across the table, and we struck up a conversation about the weather. She liked the idea of the Thoreau walk when I told her about it, then asked if I was hungry, and invited me back to her house for smoked salmon and bagels. She first showed me the patch of marijuana that she and her wife were growing in the back garden, where I spent some time sipping a second cup of coffee and watching the leaves of her pot plants wave in the wind, under the sunshine. After breakfast, we made a cardboard sign that read *Nauset*, where my car was hopefully still parked. Mary painted pink tulips around the lettering.

"People would be crazy to not give you a ride with that kind of sign," she said.

LOON ON THE BEACH

I easily found a ride back to Nauset. The driver and I made small talk. Not a single remarkable or memorable thing happened in the thirty minutes it took to cover the distance I'd just walked.

A week of black, amnesiac sleep followed my homecoming. Exactly what I wanted—to be obliterated by the insistent presence of the sea, as the sea had done to Cape Cod.

Interlude I

After a week of dreamless nights following my Cape walk, the nightmares returned. When they woke me, usually around 2:00 AM, I'd go to the kitchen. I'd made a habit of boiling water just for something to do. I'd watch the jittering blue-flower flame under the pot, kill it when the pot whistled, then listen to the heat crackle up through the metal.

I googled "dream hypnosis," found someone local named Leah. Her website advertised that she'd helped over fifteen hundred people in her practice, treating anxiety, insomnia, smoking, procrastination, PTSD, relationship issues, fatigue, and all types of phobias. I made an appointment for her first available opening.

I arrived at Leah's office in the early morning. She had pale blue eyes, a hard line of bangs, and the breezy confidence and constant smile that gave her the authority of someone who has a secret. She smiled as she listened to me explain that I wanted to stop dreaming.

"Bad dreams?" she said softly, like a song. "We can solve that in one session. Do you want to pay now or later?"

I paid her right then. The five therapists that I had seen in the two years before had all told me, in the first session, that any progress would take months.

I sat in a leather recliner. She dimmed the lights. A water fountain shaped like a rocky landscape gurgled in the corner.

"Close your eyes," she said. "Are you comfortable?"

I nodded, then I heard what sounded like her snapping all her fingers on her thumbs, a drumming flutter, just above my face.

"You are falling," she said.

She said that I was dropping somewhere, deeper and deeper, and then asked me to try to open my eyes.

"I can't," I said, astonished. I raised my eyebrows to lift my eyelids. Nothing.

"Good. Now go to a time and place in your past where you feel at home. Where is home? Where is a safe placc?"

I was still trying to open my eyelids, amazed that this was real, that with a few hand flutters she had blinded me. I wondered how small the muscles of an eyelid were—a fingernail-width? How much could an eyelid weigh?

"Tell me where you are," she said, sounding a bit impatient.

I was not hypnotized, I didn't think—I was conscious and aware of her body close to mine, could hear her breath and the sound of her chair creaking as she shifted. Embarrassment started to settle in. My face flushed. I squirmed in the chair.

I breathed, tried to think what *a safe place* meant. Where was most home. I understood what she was asking, but at the time—feeling her stare, the closeness of her body, the electric whir of the motor pumping water down the fake stones of the fountain—my mind was desolate.

"Tell me where you are," she said again. I shut my eyes tighter. A minute passed. More.

"Tell me where you are," she insisted.

I thought of my childhood home, of the smell of the wood beams, of the antique eel spears that my dad collected and nailed to the walls, of the fireplace chimney that my brother and I would shoot fireworks up, of our dachshund lying in the irises outside the kitchen window and how when he died we'd buried him right there, by those irises, and how that was the first and only time I'd seen my dad cry. Through his tears, my dad said of our dachshund, "He was my friend." I thought of the room where I used to do my homework after school, of seeing a sparrow fly into the room one warm spring day when all the doors and windows were open. From that room, I watched geese thread the sky, starlings move over the fallow farm fields like black cloth coming apart. Most memories of home, I thought in the hypnotist's office, were linked to birds—to the many that arrived in the summer and the few that remained in the winter. After coming home from school, in the fall, I'd sometimes go out bird-watching with my mom. There was a time, when I was ten or eleven, walking with her to the salt marsh, when we heard the wheezing, rhythmic sounds of two tundra swans. Whistling swans, they're also called. They had just lifted from the water and were shooting toward us. We knelt as the swans hovered closer—so close that, as I remember it, I saw their muscles moving in their chests. The sound of them—that musical gasp timed with the wingbeats—closed in, and then exploded right overhead.

NUMBER 35, LEAH'S OFFICE

"I'm in the marsh," I told Leah. "With two swans right over my head."

"Good," she said. "When you have bad dreams, ask your mind to take you back there."

Mount Katahdin: *This Ground Is Not Prepared for You*

June. I'd been feeling as if my head was underwater for about a month. I fell over once because the floor was tilting, and had random fevers through the days. My elbows and shoulder hurt. At first, I thought it was because of my sleeplessness, but I went to the doctor anyway. She took blood, and called later to say it was Lyme disease and to prescribe doxycycline—an antibiotic that makes your skin burn under the sun and pillages your gut. Weeks into taking it, I was napping two or three times a day, staying awake and sweating at night, and never really going outside anymore, except after dark, when I didn't want to lie awake in bed or had already boiled water. In the following weeks, I started confusing my left and right hands. My arms tingled. I'd stand in the kitchen, wondering what it was I had come in there to get. I shuffled around one morning with coffee, trying to remember the capital of Northern Ireland. I had hours of fatigue and forgetfulness and sleeplessness that would eventually lead to three and a half months of the doxycycline and a sort of despondency I thought would unfurl forever.

All the same, I had an upcoming artist-in-residence program to attend in Maine, and I didn't want to miss it. Two years earlier, I'd gone up to Gates of the Arctic National Park in northern Alaska to make watercolor paintings of tundra wildflowers—a project that led to a residency at the Schoodic Institute in Acadia National Park, Maine, on a peninsula across from Mount Desert Island, to paint coastal flora.

I packed my watercolors, a duffel, my bottles of doxycycline, and headed north.

"I never saw the tick bite," I told my friend Ben, a traveling musician who was visiting me in Acadia, on his way through Maine. "Now I have an excuse for looking like I never sleep."

We were hiking up a hill on Mount Desert Island, and my limbs felt like they were filled with honey. We arrived at a granite outcropping, overlooking a pan of sparkling, cold Maine water.

"You actually don't look so good," he said. "You're really pale. Should you go to the doctor again?"

"I have bacteria living in my eyes and joints," I said. "So—I don't feel so good."

We continued along a ridgeline, past windbeaten evergreens.

"You've hiked up Mount Katahdin, right?" I asked.

He had climbed most mountains north of Boston. Katahdin is the tallest peak in Maine and the one that, in September of 1846, Henry attempted to summit—three years before walking along Cape Cod.

"I have," he said. "Why?"

It had been five weeks since I'd gone to the Cape, back in May. I wanted another walk. I wanted to be led to something like another laser show, to meet someone like another Dora, to have my mind swept.

I explained my Cape walk, and that maybe I'd try to follow another Thoreau walk.

"I'm in Maine anyway," I said. "So I figured I'd head to Katahdin."

"Well," Ben said, "I'm not going to say you shouldn't do that hike now, but you shouldn't. But if you do, you have to make a parking reservation at the base of the mountain."

We finished our walk, returned to his car.

"Good luck," he said when he dropped me back off at the Institute. "Just bring a phone in case you need an airlift."

I laughed, and he didn't.

Back in my apartment, I made an Airbnb reservation in Millinocket, the gateway town to Mount Katahdin, and then walked outside with my watercolors in the evening light, looking around my feet for flowers to paint. Even though it was the height of summer, near the solstice, the Institute appeared abandoned. On the day that I arrived, the artist-in-residence coordinator told me that the art classes I was looking forward to teaching had been canceled. That was good, she insisted, because it gave me "lots of free time to myself." The weeks following, I would see a few people a day, an ecologist or administrator scurrying along the paths connecting the campus buildings, and nobody else. I'd envisioned a cafeteria where I'd meet biologists, exchange ideas about the intersection of art and science, like the research stations I'd seen in documentaries about Antarctica, but there was no such cafeteria: I had received an email the day before I arrived saying, "You are responsible for your own food." So there I sat in my apartment every night, alone, eating spaghetti or frozen pizza, the dark hours on an empty campus spread out long before me. I sometimes went to walk the streets of Winter Harbor, a town twenty minutes away with a population of a few hundred, which had a vibrant Lobster Festival that would take place a couple of months after I left.

All this meant that I had lots of time to myself, just as the coordinator said. Mostly, I spent nights reading the nearly five-hundred-page *The Maine Woods*, by Henry David Thoreau, which I'd optimistically brought along.

"I stand in awe of my body," he wrote in the Mount Katahdin section.

I read at the kitchen table, under a plank of fluorescent light.

"This matter to which I am bound has become so strange to me. I fear not spirits, ghosts, of which I am one,—*that* my body might,—but I fear bodies, I tremble to meet them. What is this Titan that has possession of me? Talk of mysteries! Think of our life in nature,—daily to be shown matter, to come in contact with it,—rocks, trees, wind on our cheeks! the *solid* earth! the *actual* world! the *common sense*! *Contact! Contact! Who* are we? *where* are we?"

I took a blue pill of doxycycline, less enthusiastic about my body, and went to bed.

Henry was famously ill twice. The first was in the winter of 1842, at twenty-four years old, when his older brother, John, cut himself while sharpening a razor, developed lockjaw, and died from tetanus ten days later. Henry developed psychosomatic lockjaw, which turned so bad that his family thought he'd also die. I realized long after I read that fact that 1842 was the year Henry took the first of his famous walks—when he stepped out his front door in Concord and ambled all the way to Wachusett Mountain, forty or so miles west. Was he walking for loss? Did he want to sleep somewhere else for a few nights, listen to the slush of autumn crickets and meet only strangers and be a little hungry for the next meal and be lulled into reverie by the simple fact that all he had to do that day was keep walking?

His second famous illness was tuberculosis, which ended up killing him at forty-four years old—which still reads to me more like a recording error than the actual age that this timelessly elegant writer, with his sage-like eyes and graying beard, died.

Henry took over a week to get to the base of Mount Katahdin from his home in Massachusetts; I left the

Institute after lunch and got there by midafternoon. Mosquitoes stuck by the hundreds to my windshield. I'd taken the back roads, because they were prettier, intersecting towns with general stores still in business. Near Bangor I stopped for a crossing snapping turtle. When it didn't move, I parked in the center of the road, put on my blinkers, and, with a stick I snapped from a tree, poked at it, because helping animals cross roads suggests luck, I've found. In the ten minutes it took to get the turtle across, the mosquitoes managed to bite even my nostril and eyelid.

"I'm calling about your stay tonight," my Airbnb host, Bob, said over the phone, while I was still driving north. Bob had double-booked—would I mind staying in another house?

"No problem," I said.

"You'll love it," he said.

At sunset, I met Bob in Millinocket at the new address he'd texted. It was a pretty, small cottage near train tracks that cut through the old mill town. The houses were lined up side by side, but with more wildness in their lawns than what you see in today's cramped suburbia.

Bob was a head taller than me, with leathery tanned skin, a gray goatee, and blue, catlike eyes. He

HOUSE OF THE DECEASED MAN

smiled as he listened to me talk about the drive up, about the snapping turtle. He was missing a finger, and, ever since I'd lost the tip of my middle finger in an accident, I liked anyone who also had a bit of his hand missing.

"I just bought this house from the bank," Bob said, walking inside with me. "The guy who owned it died a couple months ago."

I wasn't sure how to feel about a fact like that, but I appreciated Bob's honesty. I knew that I didn't want to be someone who'd get scared away by a death. Plus, if I saw a ghost, I could finally believe that there was more to the world than what was in front of me.

We walked into the bedroom, which contained not a bed but a hospital gurney. Writing this now, after the fact, I had to look up *gurney* to make sure it was the right word—that the object wasn't a hospital cot. It was, indeed, a gurney, wheels and all.

"You're the first one to sleep here!" Bob said excitedly. "Just had the carpets redone," he added, pointing to the floor.

I stood in the room filled with weak sunlight. I looked at the bed a man had likely died in, or at least had been nearly dead in.

"Going up the mountain tomorrow?" he asked.

"Trying," I said.

"It's easy," he said. "But you need to wake up early. Here." He opened the drawer to the bedside table and pulled out a digital clock. He plugged it into the wall, asked what time I was hoping to start the hike. He set the clock, checking it against his wristwatch.

We shook hands. He said thanks for being so flexible. I said not to worry about it.

After Bob left, I sat on the gurney, pressed the firm mattress, lifted my feet, and lay down to test it. A ridgeline cut through its center, and therefore my spine. When I turned to find a more comfortable position, the sheets crackled, and I realized that there was a plastic covering on the mattress, the kind for bed-wetting trouble. When I hesitantly smelled the covers, they gave off the aroma of laundry detergent.

For their own bed the night before they hiked Katahdin, Henry and his companions cut cedar twigs from the forest. As one of them "lopped off the smallest twigs of the flat-leaved cedar, the arbor-vitae of the gardens, we gathered them up, and returned with them to the boat, until it was loaded. Our bed was made with as much care and skill as a roof is shingled; beginning at the foot, and laying the twig end of the cedar upward, we advanced to the head, a course at a time, thus successively covering the stub-ends, and producing a soft and level bed."

Mine was neither soft nor level—the gurney, which had an electric controller that could lift the upper half to a sitting position, was stuck at an angle sloped just a few degrees up.

I went looking for dinner.

Henry ate fish he caught in a nearby stream: "That these jewels," he wrote of the fish, "should have swam away in that Aboljacknagesic water for so long, so many dark ages;—these bright fluviatile flowers, seen of Indians only, made beautiful, the Lord only knows why, to swim there!" He drank a cup of water, which he called "condensed cloud."

Everything on the menu of the restaurant I went to—a mile out of town, pocketed in a cluster of towering evergreens—was meat-filled. At the time I was in one of my vegetarian phases, prompted by a hard note of guilt after spending a day with my neighbors' piglets.

"Spaghetti, please," I told the waitress, "without the meatballs."

"Sausage instead?" she asked.

"No, thanks," I said.

And because I was afraid of drinking alcohol with the antibiotic, I ordered a water.

"Pasta with just sauce," she said. "And water?"

I nodded. She shook her head as if I'd done something wrong. I should have just gone to the market, but I'd wanted to get out of the dead man's house. With nobody to talk with, I watched the same baseball game playing on two side-by-side televisions over the bar. It was hypnotic to watch them together: the running players identically sliding diagonally up the two screens; the two baseballs streaking down the centers; the two close-ups of the pitcher's face, nodding and twitching and turning to look for the lead on first. As hypnotic as watching a flock of birds moving together.

The pasta came, covered in watery tomato sauce that tasted like iodine.

"Supper was eaten off a large log," Henry wrote, "which some freshet had thrown up. This night we had a dish of arbor-vitae or cedar tea, which the lumberer sometimes uses when other herbs fail." He then relaxed beside a blazing fire. "In the night I dreamed of trout-fishing," he wrote.

I returned to the house and prepared for bed. Took a shower in the dead man's shower, used one of the dead man's towels, brushed my teeth in front of the mirror and thought how he'd probably stood right there,

DINNER IN MILLINOCKET

looking at his reflection for years, until a few months ago. Now it was my reflection. I suppose that's a neat little summary of passing life: that at some point your face is replaced by another's. That where you stood at your sink to brush your teeth is now the place where another stands. Your empty seat, taken.

Lying in the gurney with my eyes closed, anxious I wasn't falling asleep because I'd have to wake before dawn and drive to the mountain and hike up and back down in one day while on two daily doses of an antibiotic that made my stomach cramp, I fell into a light sleep in which I dreamed of a person staring at me from the doorway of the bedroom.

A piercing shriek came hours later. I sprung up in the gurney, my heart punching my ribs, sure that it was the scream of death or the dead. The alarm clock blinked. Bob had missed it. I punched at it, couldn't find the button to shut it off, so tore it from the wall and threw it on the floor. I panted. My legs washed with the cold prickling you get from a nearly missed car accident.

I spent most of the night sitting on the couch in the living room—which was, it turned out, more comfortable than the gurney. I heard a faraway train whistle, underlining the silence of the wilderness that spread for a hundred miles in every direction.

The next day, before noon, I was above the tree line, wind blowing in from Canada, distant mountains powder blue in atmosphere. The hike had been easier than I expected, coming up the same side of the mountain Henry had taken. A well-worn path reminded me that I was walking to a tourist destination and not, as I might have wanted to believe, into the wilderness. Steps helped me up harder parts. Vibrant markers kept me on the trail. Wooden planks kept my feet dry over the wet areas. And then there were the tourists themselves: the tinny sound of music from a phone strapped to the arm of a guy with two hiking poles; a couple, mid-fight, on the side of the path, the woman sitting down and the man hovering over her while he threw up his arms and she told him to just keep walking; the group of high schoolers wearing rain jackets on this overcast but not rainy day, and who together made the sound of a hundred plastic bags. At one point on his own walk, Henry was "startled" to see a footprint beside a stream they'd passed on the way up—disbelieving that there could be another traveler in such deep wilderness. It turned out to be a footprint from his own walking group, left hours earlier.

The clouds parted and the sun hatched through. I sat down and wrote in my notebook, *Would love to*

*have the thoughts of the firs traded for my own. Snow /
ice / sun.*

"It was vast," Henry wrote of the mountain's summit.
"Titanic, and such as man never inhabits. Some part
of the beholder, even some vital part, seems to escape
through the loose grating of his ribs as he ascends.
He is more lone than you can imagine. There is less
of substantial thought and fair understanding in him
than in the plains where men inhabit . . . [Nature]
seems to say sternly, Why came ye here before your
time. This ground is not prepared for you . . . Why
seek me where I have not called thee, and then
complain because you find me but a stepmother?
Shouldst thou freeze or starve, or shudder thy life
away, here is no shrine, nor altar, nor any access to
my ear."

"Seriously?" a guy standing beside me on the summit said, looking at his phone. "No service?"

Have we given up trying to keep the business of our
lives away from the mountains? I thought. Is firing up
FaceTime—as two others were then doing beside me—
just a fine thing to do, now? "The tops of mountains
are among the unfinished parts of the globe," Henry
thought, where it is "a slight insult to the gods to climb

and pry into their secrets, and try their effect on our humanity." This must be the limit of insulting the gods: a man waving his phone overhead.

If you've hiked to a summit in the past decade, you know that after taking a selfie, the next thing people do is eat. And so, out came the tinfoil-wrapped sandwiches, the Ziploc bags of dried fruit, the matchbox-sized raisin packs, the apples, and quantities of trail mix nobody eats on a normal day. Which is why I wanted to thank the guy who sat down beside me and brought out—amazingly—a whole avocado and a red soda.

After he sliced open the avocado, he said to his friend, speaking of the soda, "The raspberry flavor comes from a gland. It's all natural."

"It's a chemical," the friend said. "That's why it says 'artificial flavoring.'"

"No," he said, scooping out chunks of avocado with a white plastic spoon. "It comes from a beaver's butthole. All natural."

He was in his midtwenties, with long, black banana curls that danced in the wind roaring over the summit. He wore the same type of thick-rimmed glasses as Dora, and had not a scrap of hiking gear—only khaki shorts and a torn flannel shirt. What was he doing here? Why had he come to the summit—drawn by what curiosity or what requirement?

The wind gathered the end of their beaver-and-flavor conversation away from me. He then stood, foot up on a rock and knee bent.

"That's the thing about being an adult," he said. "You realize you have control over things like ball sweat. You don't have to wait for your mom to take you to the mall to buy your Under Armour. You can just buy it yourself."

I suddenly felt very tired. I walked down to the other side of the summit, to a place overlooking the famous Knife Edge trail. I swallowed my second antibiotic pill of the day, then found a flat rock to rest on. I breathed in the stone's gunpowder scent. The wind pushed away the mosquitoes. The sun warmed my skin. Sleep was coming, led by the little electrical pops behind my eyes that, I've been told, also accompany Lyme.

Then I heard her: the teen who would eventually drive me from the summit as the rainstorm drove Henry from it.

"I'm. Not. Having. Fun!" she screamed.

I sat up, startled from the edge of sleep. She was a hundred feet away, sitting on a boulder. Both her parents were standing over her, leaning in. They didn't see me, because I was mostly hidden behind a stone.

"The summit is right up there, honey," the father said. "The end is close."

"You're lying!" she screamed. Actually screamed. Though, yes, you could see—anyone could see—that the summit really was right up there, no more than a couple hundred feet.

The father and mother looked at each other. The girl folded her arms, put her head down. For a moment, they looked peaceful, almost like one of those old Renaissance paintings of a family gathered in silent prayer on a mountainside. A divine moment. Awaiting grace. The only sound, at the time, was the rocks cutting up the north wind.

"Do you want your sandwich now?" the father asked.

She only screamed then. Metallic in texture and from her throat. No words.

"Just go," the mother said to the father. "Go."

He turned, walked away, toward the mountaintop. The mother did, too, after sitting for some time with the daughter.

"Stay here," the mother said to her. "We'll be down in fifteen minutes."

KATAHDIN SUMMIT

"I must receive my life as passively as the willow leaf that flutters over the brook," Henry once wrote, which might be advice for this girl or, more, for her parents.

Before the mother was very far, the girl ran after them.

This was the moment—not suburban developments or roads—that felt to be the widest chasm between my own experience and Henry's. Here was a family, ambling safely up Maine's highest peak, their greatest worry being whether one member is having fun and if a sandwich would help that fun. It felt then as though nothing was untouched by people.

"I was deep within the hostile ranks of clouds," Henry wrote about his time here. "And all objects were obscured by them. Now the wind would blow me out a yard of clear sunlight, wherein I stood."

I hiked up the summit for one last look. The family was up there, all eating their sandwiches. The girl looked happy, ripping her sandwich into many pieces and swaying as—I saw her headphones then—she listened to music. The parents stared separately into the distance, to the bluish mountains and the expanse of lakes in a valley made by a glacier tens of thousands of years ago. They looked a little stunned, a little tired, maybe pensive, maybe struck by the immensity of the wilderness seen over their daughter's head bobbing to notes only she could hear.

"Perhaps," Henry wrote when he descended, "I most fully realized that this was primeval, untamed, and forever untamable *Nature*, or whatever else men call it, while coming down this part of the mountain." Beyond the horizon of his wilderness was the automobile, roadways that cut into the deepest part of the country, internet and phones that would make travel to the mountain in a day easy, heating and air-conditioning, caretakers cutting paths and the thousands of people stepping on those paths every year. Maybe he couldn't imagine the numbers of us, the billions tending and misusing and witnessing the same earth he walked on, the way that by our numbers we created a wave to breach into the farthest reaches of landscape. What wave of progress or technology is beyond my horizon? I thought, starting down from the summit. Will this all be ruined so slowly that I won't recognize it as ruin, only change?

On my way down, I passed the guy with banana curls climbing over boulders. I thought of asking him about the beaver. It might not be the same sort of wildness that Henry experienced on Katahdin, but a berry flavor in the asshole of a semiaquatic, tree-eating, river-stopping giant rodent is a mystery of the American wilderness that I wanted to believe in just then.

I returned to Schoodic by nightfall. I put water on to boil, saw there was a message on my phone from Kipp, my friend who lived an hour and a half down the coast, in Blue Hill. Her family ran a business that caught and shipped starfish, lampreys, sea urchins, and other marine specimens to universities for biology students to dissect. I'd met Kipp a decade earlier on an island off southern Maine, when I completed my college Field Ornithology course and an independent research project at Shoals Marine Laboratory. I spent most days in a navy jumpsuit wading through shoulder-high poison ivy, looking for common eiders' feather-made nests and creamy-mint-colored eggs, and later counting how many of their ducklings had been eaten by great black-backed gulls each day.

Kipp was the lab preparator at Shoals—laying out dead seals for anatomy lessons, organizing shipments and data sets, prepping labs for classes. She played the fiddle, I the banjo, and we both loved bird-watching. We became good friends, spent evenings on the island playing tunes. Before arriving in Schoodic, I'd written her to say that I'd be on the coast of Maine for a couple of weeks, and we should meet up sometime.

The jellyfish were "blooming" just north of Schoodic Point, she said in her voice message. Would I want to meet her and her dad tomorrow? They could pick me up on their boat.

I didn't know what a jellyfish bloom meant, or if we'd be out long, or what the weather would be like, or if there'd be any work involved, but I strongly wanted to meet an old friend and have a face-to-face conversation. So, the following morning, I stood on her dad's boat, motoring out on the cold, green water, happier than I'd been the whole week. She talked about how her beekeeping was going, her seaweed pressings, what was growing in her garden, how her new flock of sheep was doing, and how she was recently interested in "air meadows"—the long-lost tradition of feeding livestock the lopped leafy tops of trees.

"Here they come," she said, interrupting herself, pointing over the side of the boat. "You can see them rising up."

In the water, hundreds—or thousands—of pale moon jellies lifted into view. Each foggy disk was about a foot in diameter and contained four smaller circles in its center. The bloom moved together on some invisible submerged current—undulating, drifting, urged to the surface and then sinking away.

Bloom not as in a blossom, I saw, then—*bloom* as in production, as in abundance, as in plenty. A blush of jellyfish.

Kipp leaned over the gunwale, ran her net through the water, scooping up a few, then carefully deposited them in bins sloshing with preserving fluids.

We spent the morning like this. The jellies rising and falling like some huge, disembodied underwater lung. We talked in the minutes they sank beyond the reach of her net.

That night, back in my apartment, I searched online for "air meadows," but was shown only advertisements and reviews for a Febreze Air scent called "Meadows & Rain." I had gone looking for how this poetry had snuck into agriculture, for who had fused the words that made me think of animals grazing in the sky, of chewable air, only to find it dismembered on the internet's chopping block. I'd call Kipp the next morning. She'd know where it came from.

I walked outside that night, I remember, to the shoreline. I stood on the granite, looking at the black water, thinking of what was under there.

Interlude II

I'd never visited Walden, so on a hot day in August, a couple of months after Katahdin, I drove up to see the most famous pond in America.

A replica of Henry's cabin, near the parking lot, was smaller than I expected, and it took some imagination to believe that the site was once tranquil, now with the sound of nearby traffic and families heading to the pond.

I walked into the cabin, sat in a replica rocking chair beside a replica woodstove. I admit I was likely hollow-eyed, staring at nothing or at the floor—such were the days with antibiotics and Lyme disease, which had only worsened. I had a beard then, too, and long hair, because I'd given up shaving or getting haircuts under the dulling effects bad health has on grooming.

Still, I was surprised when a woman and her little son walked through the door, stopped, and she said, "Oh, look, there he is."

I've always dressed traditionally, I suppose. Most of my pants are black cotton; my shirts button-downs. I wear boots or clogs.

"Ask him a question," she said to the boy, pushing him forward, toward the reenactor she thought I was.

I briefly considered if I should try to drum up a line about growing beans or civil disobedience for the little boy, who was now walking hesitantly across the creaking wooden floor, but my mind was tired.

I held up a hand. "No," I said, smiling.

I stood, patted down my pants nervously. I skirted past the boy, strode out of the cabin, toward the pond where Henry had gone skinny-dipping. Maybe my leaving was in character, I thought, turning back to see the woman give me a look like, *What the hell?*

The pond was cerulean cellophane. The trees around its rim swayed in the midsummer wind. I sat in the sand, watching swallows picking at the surface, drinking, and then trying to snatch up a white feather that was boating across and would be good building material for a nest. To my side, an elderly man in a bathing suit was using a walker to make his way toward the water. He was alone. He moved slowly and, it looked, painfully, taking a few seconds to pause after each step. He'd then lift his walker, move it half a foot forward, and step.

There are some things you know you'll never see again, like a man shuffling into a pond with a walker, the waterline inching up to his tight grip on the handles. He then fell back, into the lap of the water. It was as close to watching somebody fly as I'll likely see. He stretched flat, arms winged out. His toes surfaced. Above him, the swallows swooped. His arm lifted overhead, and he back-paddled toward the center of the pond, moving much more swiftly than he had when gravity was holding him, leaving the walker there. I thought of the words *husk, shed, clip, unshackled.*

I took off my shirt, my shoes, my socks, and my pants. Down to my boxers. I walked into the water, past the man's walker. Little khaki-colored fish, the size of the alewives I'd seen in Wellfleet, were weaving around the walker's legs.

I swam out to where the bottom was ten or fifteen feet below. Admired how clear the pond was. Held my breath, then let it all out. I sank. Air bubbles licked my face. I opened my eyes to see blurry shafts of sunlight skewering the water. My lungs burned, but I felt good, because the deeper I went, the less my Lyme-pinched joints hurt. My feet touched the bottom. I stood there, my ears pressured, my joints relieved, in the pond where Henry went every morning. How quiet it was. In the water pressed in all around me, I now wish I could have seen that a better future was, in fact, coming. That the Lyme would eventually fade away and I would not be left with the decades-long aftereffects I feared. That I would stop feeling scared of my dreams, mostly by gathering lengths of time. That within a year after sinking into the pond, I would be the happiest I'd been in a very long time.

I swam up to the surface, my lungs burning, water in my eyes.

WALDEN

Wachusett Mountain: *The Stars Were Given for a Consolation*

Mid-October. I was lying on the grassy slopes of Wachusett Mountain, a few hours into the MDMA I'd taken, looking up at a channel of stars running between the torn edges of overarching oaks. I'd wanted to feel some of the transcendence in nature that Henry felt, and which I hadn't really yet experienced in the walking, and thought the pills might help. My body felt warm, maybe from the drug, but also because it was seventy degrees—a summer night misplaced in autumn. The katydids chirped in the trees in their one-two, in-out rhythm. "By taking the ether the other day I was convinced how far asunder a man could be separated from his senses," Henry wrote of his own drug experience when he was thirty-four. "You expand like a seed in the ground. You exist in your roots, like a tree in the winter. If you have an inclination to travel, take the ether; you go beyond the furthest star."

I'd started my walk that morning at an Audubon wildlife sanctuary about three miles from Wachusett's summit. In the nature center, I chatted with a smiley docent about monarch butterflies and black swallow-tail butterflies, and then asked her what would happen if I left my car in the center's parking lot overnight. She said overnight parking wasn't allowed.

"Just because—I want to see the sunset," I said. "And I'm not sure I'll be back before dark."

"But you're not spending the night?"

She tilted her head to look over my shoulder, to my backpack, in which I'd put a Subway sandwich for dinner and my sleeping bag for spending the night.

"Have a nice walk," she said. "And if you don't get back before nightfall, I won't call a tow truck."

The stone walls running throughout the forest near the sanctuary were a reminder that the forest was new, that the stones had been placed in one-time farm fields. All day, wind shook rain from the trees. And the clouds—a roiling mess overhead, sometimes breaking up for sunlight in a way that reminded me of Henry's writing about Katahdin—enshrouded the ski lifts that I found myself walking under. Scattered at my feet were slicks of torn mushrooms. If spring is the season for the eyes—"Earth laughs in flowers," wrote Ralph Waldo Emerson—and summer for touch—of the sun, of bare feet, of seawater on your skin—then fall is mostly for the nose: the bass-note scent of the ground. To walk through a forest in New England's autumn is to put your nose to nature's neck.

Henry walked with a friend from his home in Concord, Massachusetts, all the way to the summit, which I didn't do, because I didn't want to trudge through suburbia. I would have heard the hoarse rush of traffic, and not, as he described in his essay "A Walk to Wachusett," "the murmuring of water, and the slumberous breathing of crickets, throughout the night."

At least I expected the parking lot when I reached the summit. Still, it was a sadly distant experience from Henry's: "When we reached [the summit]," he wrote, "we felt a sense of remoteness, as if we had traveled into distant regions, to Arabia Petræa, or the farthest East." On the summit, he found blueberries, raspberries, gooseberries, strawberries, yellow lilies, and a "fine, wiry grass." I found a pond stocked with pet-store goldfish, which I would have been more disheartened to see had it not been for their iridescent beauty in the black water. A man walked from his car to the pond, holding a bag of potato chips. He saw the fish, tossed a chip into the pond. The goldfish gathered around and under the chip. "It was a place where gods might wander," Henry wrote of this summit. "So solemn and solitary, and removed from all contagion with the plain."The man finished his chips, then tipped the bag and shook it over the pond water. Crumbs fluttered to the goldfish.

Sunset cast the sky in pink clouds extending all the way to Mount Monadnock, there in the north, across the border between Massachusetts and New Hampshire. Two ravens played in the updrafts, performing beneath the clouds. The wind came from the southwest, whistling through the metalwork of the weather station near the parking lot. I pinched out the small Ziploc bag of MDMA from my coat pocket and took a pill, then sat on the weather station's lookout platform, and within the hour had a notion that the pink clouds were in my Lyme-hurt joints, which were loose and warm and soothed for the second time that summer. "My body was the organ and channel of melody, as a flute is of the music that is breathed through it," Henry wrote in his journal on an October morning, after waking from a dream.

A man with a white beard to his chest set up a spotting scope not far away. Feeling outrageously happy, I asked him what exactly he was looking for.

"Counting hawks," he said.

He had green eyes and sharp cheekbones, and wore a moss-green woolen cap.

"Been a lot of sharp-shinneds this year," I said.

He rocked back and forth, "Lot of sharp-shinneds," he said.

He explained his work: estimating the numbers of migrating birds of prey in any given "kettle"—a towering column of birds soaring on an updraft. The updrafts are made by hot air rising from parking lots or, before we paved the wilderness, stretches of stone or lakes. The hawks are lifted, he said, and then, at the top of the updraft, soar down to the next one, like taking an elevator to the top floor, riding down to the next building on a slide, and then riding up again. Hawks can make nearly the whole migration to Mexico this way.

When he said he was also counting butterflies for the state, I reasoned that I'd come across Henry David Thoreau reincarnated.

"I counted twenty-three monarchs today," he said. "Big year. But not like ten years ago. A hundred in a day."

FIRE TOWER, SUMMIT

His white beard jittered in the wind. He squinted, lifted his binoculars, rested them again. Scratched at his soft green hat.

"Dragonflies, too," he said. "I've been counting those."

We looked out to landscape spread like the ocean in front of us.

"How ample and roomy is nature," Henry wrote from this same vantage.

A man with a gray and tremendous mustache appeared at the bird-watcher's side. He leaned forward and said to me, "He counts everything. I'm new to this."

He reached over and introduced himself. "Paul," he said. "From Michigan."

"That's a long way away," I said.

"I live here now. With my girlfriend." Paul said he and his girlfriend knew each other from high school, when his family lived here before moving to the Midwest. "We were in band class together."

As the expert hawk-counter wandered off to the other side of the platform, Paul told me about the wonders of the Upper Peninsula. The MDMA was making it hard to concentrate, but the general notion I got was that he missed it.

"This place," Paul said, pointing to the ground, to the mountain we shared then, "I come here every day. I'm addicted to it. Sometimes I say to myself, 'I don't have time for this,' but I always come."

He then described the drive from his house to the mountain. I don't think I responded, but do remember thinking how kind his eyes looked—down-turned and topped with feral gray eyebrows. For reasons I can't remember I asked if he was Polish, to which he looked confused and then carried on about his preferred route to Wachusett, and how different it was from the Upper Peninsula in elevation and forest type. He was plainly homesick. Here he was, looking out at the slosh of pink clouds, and all he could talk about was Detroit, as it used to be.

I told him he'd love Massachusetts, as if he hadn't already lived here. I then told him I had to leave, and wandered off the lookout, paused and turned and waved goodbye to him and the bird-watcher, and meandered from the summit to the top of the chairlift. The metal chair—a big four-seater—creaked in the wind. I walked up the off-ramp people usually ski down.

Sitting on the chair, I watched a porcupine amble from a tree's foot, part the grass with its brambly body, and eat a yellow flower. "These bristly fellows are a very suitable small fruit of such unkempt wilder-nesses," wrote Henry of a porcupine.

I heard barking, and turned to see a man pulling a brown-and-black blotted mutt by a leash. The dog, smelling the porcupine, reared up. Behind the man, two boys came running down from the summit, and circled in front of the dog. The boys must have been ten or eleven, each holding a stick, their boots and socks and shins mud-splattered.

"Careful," I called to the man. "There's a porcupine here."

"Whoa, whoa, whoa!" he yelled at the dog, yanking him back.

The boys kept running, pounding up the ramp.

"Where?" one of the boys asked me.

I pointed down the hill. They crept forward and sat on the wooden boards beside the chair.

The three of us watched the porcupine graze. One of the boys sat with both legs drawn up to his chest, arms hugging his dirty shins. The other sat cross-legged, enraptured.

"I've never seen a porky-pine," one of the boys said, so quietly he nearly whispered.

The dog let out a long howl. The father dug his heels into the ground. The boys knew it was bad if the dog got to the porcupine, and were also, I think, interested by the possibility of it, by the fact that something violent and painful might happen any moment. And so there was tension: the dog pulling on the leash; the porcupine softly licking up the stem of a flower, easy in its armor. And between those two animals, the boys, wanting, perhaps, for the dog to break away from their father. Waiting to see what would happen when the dog's face punched the porcupine.

The sound of the chairs' crooked metal arms squeaking on the metal cable named that tension as the train whistle in Millinocket named its solitude.

"Let's go!" the father yelled to the boys.

One boy left immediately, rushing toward the father, who was already pulling the dog down the slope. The other boy stayed by the chairlift a moment. Again, he said to himself—for whom else could he be talking to?—"I've never seen a porky-pine."

He might think about this evening from time to time in his life, of the porcupine eating flowers—an animal of a rarity that casts the landscape in possibility, that really anything could walk out of the woods. I imagined him older, maybe twenty years from now, driving home from work, seeing a porcupine on the road. He might stop the car to watch it slowly cross. He might think back to now, the first time he'd seen one, how he'd been sitting on a chairlift over a meadowy ski slope, how he'd been on a walk with his brother and dad and their dog. He might remember me, vaguely—a stranger also looking at the porcupine. The memory might give him the sensation of his childhood floating back to him, unexpectedly, as my own childhood comes to me whenever I smell skunk cabbage, which grew on the roadside streambed where my best friend and I used to play. Twenty years from now, this boy might tell someone about the porcupine he saw and about the first time he saw one when he was a boy. But he might not, out of the hesitation that comes with strong memories from early childhood—how they always sound smaller, softer, than the personality-crafting forms they really are.

The boy then stood to run after his father and brother and dog.

There's a heart inside that animal, my mind told me, watching the porcupine move down the slope, back to the edge of the forest. Maybe the size of a chestnut. There's a heart at the center of all animals. Everything is soft underneath. *A very suitable small fruit.*

After sunset, I watched the stars. The warm air shook the oak leaves overhead. I'd taken off my shoes and put my legs inside my sleeping bag. The uneven ground is an old bed that I love. Swaddled in a sleeping bag, there is no cozier place to spend time between sunset and sunrise. The dreams had been visiting me less now, four months after Cape Cod. Maybe once or twice a week, and by then, they seemed not to matter much.

The stars, the ones between the channel of silhouetted oak canopies, must be a constellation, I thought. Unlike Henry, I didn't know the names of any constellations save the Big Dipper and Orion. I had my phone, though, with a constellation app on it.

I first saw the Southern Cross, through the earth. Replicated digital stars washed through the screen as I lifted it overhead. I pointed the phone to the brightest ones.

A figure then appeared, drawn by the connecting star-points. *Cygnus*, the caption below read: "The Swan."

What to do with something so fateful that *coincidence* doesn't seem like a fair word? What to do with the hypnotist's prediction that only under the Swan I'd feel at home?

The heart of the Swan, the star called Deneb, is one of the brightest stars in the night sky, I read on the phone's screen. It is two hundred times larger than our sun.

Before sleeping on Wachusett Mountain, Henry also looked up at the stars, and also found comfort: "It was a satisfaction to know that they were our fellow-travelers still, as high and out of our reach as our own destiny. Truly the stars were given for a consolation to man. We should not know but our life were fated to be always groveling, but it is permitted to behold them, and surely they are deserving of a fair destiny. We see laws which never fail, of whose failure we never conceived; and their lamps burn all the night, too, as well as all day,—so rich and lavish is that nature which can afford this superfluity of light."

Henry had walked to Wachusett, sat up on the summit and looked at the stars as if they were "given for a consolation" six months after his brother died. Was he doing the same thing I was doing? Walking to husk the dead skin of grief? Looking up to feel the comfort of one's own smallness in the world, to displace bulging selfhood, under the shadow of such urgent beauty as the night sky? To force loss or confusion microscopic in perspective?

I spread myself on the snowless hill, and heard in my drug-slippery head, "I've never seen a porky-pine."

It came like a chant. "I've never seen a porky-pine." I wondered then if the porcupine was asleep, and what dreams she might be having. And if the boy was asleep. And his family dog. And my parents. And Mary. And Dora. And the goldfish. And Randy and Pat in Wellfleet. What weird worlds they were all inhabiting, in their dreams—tortured or hopeful or anxious or in love, but all completely alone. And then I saw it: that a large portion of the world just then was simply held in their imaginations. Billions of animals suspended in hallucinations, in some place between memory and thought. These hours named sleep, this necessary dark territory we enter alone, is a more startling spell than I can describe.

SLEEPING ON THE SKI SLOPE

Home: *Treading Old Lessons*

October passed. The sunlight was put away by late November. The birds left the landscape. The leaves changed, then crisped, then blew away and collected around the foot of my house. The buffleheads arrived. A fox made a den in a cedar copse at the end of a spit of land. Storms came and went. The gulls stayed, flying over the salt marsh. The first snow fell wet. I did house chores. I built a fire every night. Ate dinner with my parents.

Here is Henry David Thoreau on the meaning of walking, from the conclusion of his Wachusett essay: "There is, however, this consolation to the most way-worn traveler, upon the dustiest road, that the path his feet describe is so perfectly symbolical of human life,—now climbing the hills, now descending into

CYGNUS

the vales. From the summits he beholds the heavens and the horizon, from the vales he looks up to the heights again. He is treading his old lessons still, and though he may be very weary and travel-worn, it is yet sincere experience."

And here is mine, from the final pages of the notebook I took to Wachusett: *If we can't be sure of divinity, we can be sure by the divine feeling of being held in a web of love.*

I surely wrote that when the drugs were cresting, right after I saw the constellation of a swan overhead and thought the stars were speaking to me. I'm embarrassed by the hyperbole of it, but the more I look at the phrase, now, the more evidence I see in it. Like, you walk through a pine forest at dusk and a friendly couple helps you cross a pond, feeds you dinner, makes you a cup of coffee in the morning, and wishes you well on the rest of your way. You walk, rain-soaked, into a bar, and an enigmatic millionaire buys you dinner. A man in Millinocket tries to set an alarm clock for you. A novice hawk-watcher on Wachusett Mountain unravels with homesickness for the Midwest, talks of his newfound love in the second half of his life. Henry went on his walks to find the veins connecting him to nature; I went to shed my dreams. Instead of shedding,

I'd added more. More people and more landscape and more stars. How lucky it felt, like the high tide had come into my life.

So rich and lavish is that nature which can afford this superfluity of light, I think now, whenever I look up in the blue sky and am reminded of the stars behind. Only when the sun has gone down, when the darkness comes like a swipe of death over the day, do the stars show themselves. Only in darkness, seen.

I can remember that when I was very young I used to have a dream night after night, over and over again, which might have been named Rough and Smooth. All existence, all satisfaction and dissatisfaction, all event was symbolized in this way. Now I seemed to be lying and tossing, perchance, on a horrible, a fatal rough surface, which must soon, indeed, put an end to my existence, though even in the dream I knew it to be the symbol merely of my misery; and then again, suddenly, I was lying on a delicious smooth surface, as of a summer sea, as of gossamer or down or softest plush, and life was such a luxury to live. My waking experience always has been and is such an alternate Rough and Smooth.

—Henry David Thoreau, January 7, 1857

Prelude to Part Two

For a while—weeks, maybe—I tried to write about how we met, but never got it right. It all sounded too plain, too factual. Anyway, Jenny did it better in her own book, *Little Weirds*: "When I went farther up into the Arctic Circle with my friend and her sweetheart," she wrote, "we met another friend of theirs. He was tall and had dark hair and I enjoyed talking to him but I could never really look him in the eye for a number of reasons. He made an apple pie, roasted a chicken, drove the car, painted me a picture of a small blue flower, and said my name when calling me over to look at a horse that he knew I was not happy about. He told me lines from a poem that he heard in a dream."

The poem came in a dream days before I arrived in Norway. In it, I met a woman beside a canal. *Our friends pray for us*, the final line of the poem went. The blue flower was a bluebell that I'd found on one of my hikes in the fjords, and had put in a little glass jar on the dining room table in the house where we stayed.

We were all in Norway because Jenny's friend Rebecca—her *sweetheart* was my friend John—had written a screenplay that was set in the Norwegian Arctic. Jenny—a comedian, writer, and actress—was the lead in the film. They were meeting to talk about the movie and visit locations in the Lofoten Islands, a place of obvious beauty where the mountain-islands slope mythically into the sea. John had invited me to join.

Oddly, I'd nearly met Jenny many years earlier, when I went to her apartment in Brooklyn for a New Year's Eve party as a friend of a friend. There was a moment when I was standing in the middle of her living room, holding a beer and not talking to anyone, and I turned to see her standing there, by my shoulder, also, briefly, not talking to anyone. I recognized her because she was on *Saturday Night Live* at the time. I felt drawn toward her, as if my shoulder were being touched by warm pressure. I ignored the urge to say hello. I didn't want to bother her, and so turned away and left the party soon thereafter to have a snowball fight with my friends in the street.

After Jenny left Norway, I climbed the surrounding fjords by myself, to give my friends—the sweethearts—time alone. I sat on a steep slab of wet grass high above the cottage we were staying in, looking at sheep scattered across the fjord's deep scoop, inexplicably missing Jenny, this stranger I'd spent only three days with. I missed her as if she were a longtime friend, or like homesickness. I missed her and then thought how stupid it was to miss someone I didn't know, and then later found myself in the quiet kitchen in the Norwegian cottage, staring at the teakettle long after it had boiled, lost in thought. Something was missing, as sudden and big as if the ocean out the window were gone. There were three of us in the cottage; there should be four.

When I left the Arctic days after Jenny had gone, I returned to Amsterdam, where I'd been living for a year. That week, a Dutch friend asked me what it had been like up there, in the long days. I said that I felt like I'd gone up a mountain and seen the gods, surprising myself that I phrased it that way.

"Careful," he said.

We were sitting outside, at his favorite restaurant. Light reflected off the nearby canal, giving the sensation that I had often in Amsterdam: that the sun was everywhere. I felt light and cheery, sipping beer with the intention of ordering another one.

"Careful?" I asked.

"You know what happens when a mortal sees the gods?" he said.

"What?"

"You get turned into a laurel tree." He smirked. "Or a pond."

Over a year after meeting Jenny in Norway, I had moved back to Massachusetts, and we'd kept in touch. She was finishing her book at her parents' house on Martha's Vineyard, across the bay from my house, close enough that it was easy for us to meet up for an afternoon. So, one autumn day, I drove to Woods Hole and boarded the ferry.

I saw her across the water, at sea level, dressed in monochrome because, as she said, she wanted to be one color on the outside and every color on the inside. We went to the grocery store, walked in a graveyard, and agreed that most relationships end badly. We were going to be good friends, we said, on a beach walk. In our bathing suits, we walked into a sea nearly too cold for swimming. If we'd waited only days longer, I thought, we would have missed our chance.

THREE SHEEP, NORWAY

Winter came. I went to California to visit her, and never left. In her garden were lemon trees whose blossoms perfumed the air. Along the path to an old wooden shed that I used as a painting studio were clementine, tangerine, kumquat, and orange trees. When the month was right, I picked the fruit and called my brother, in Wisconsin, to say that I had just picked a clementine off a tree, in January, and was eating it, in January, and that Southern California wasn't at all what I'd expected, wasn't only the traffic and overheated days, as I'd heard. "It's actually really, really nice out here," I told him. Jenny and I drank coffee every morning at the edge of her garden, watching a ruby-throated hummingbird lick flowers. Everything smelled like citrus. The hummingbird made a nest by a window, laid eggs small as green peas. The Mexican mint marigolds bloomed, and the air around the porch smelled liked spun sugar at night.

Half a year later, in August, I took Jenny to visit my great-aunt in southern France. We'd just gone back to Norway, to the sweethearts', John and Rebecca's, wedding in a barony in a fjord, which felt something like a full circle, like a season, because here we were, Jenny and I, back in Norway, as a couple.

One day in Provence, after lunch under a grape arbor with my great-aunt, Jenny and I went to the

Saint-Rémy market to collect food for a picnic, then swam under a Roman aqueduct, then drove to the tiny village where my great-aunt had once lived in a stone house, downhill from an eleventh-century castle, for many years. We walked up the winding stone streets, under an archway of fiery bougainvillea, to the castle at the top of the hill. As we stood at the castle's gate, we watched a black goat and a white goat edge their way along a cliff, side by side. "An omen," Jenny said. We walked through the castle gates.

We set out the picnic of olives and cheeses and breads and a bottle of wine on stone steps that wound up to an archway. Sunlight raked across the village's pink and orange rooftops and on the stones at our backs that had been placed by a worker's hands so many centuries ago. The castle walls were peach colored and radiating warmth. From the picnic basket, I took out a box I'd made from an oak tree limb I'd cut from the forest behind our house, and which I'd kept secretly in my bag. My great-grandmother's ring was inside it. I held it for some moments before Jenny saw it in my hands.

This is all to say, the second half of this book was written years after I slept on Wachusett Mountain, after

I saw the Swan constellation. Things had changed. I was engaged. The anxiety and claustrophobic distress I had felt the morning I drove to Cape Cod were now a memory, packaged away somewhere in my mind that excluded the emotion of it.

In the beginning, I walked for distraction, to give myself an assignment, to escape the weight of my days. Others might go to the gym, or train for a marathon, or drive across the country. Years later, I was still reading Henry David Thoreau, and I found myself still wanting to follow him.

When I started writing this second half, Jenny was a part of it, but the urgency to leave home wasn't. But if I've learned one thing from reading Henry's journals, it's that stepping out your front door gives an offering in all seasons and moods. Something would come from continuing to follow him. So, I picked three journeys from my reading: I'd go southwest from home; I'd paddle to the farthest point north in Henry's Maine trips, and I'd return to Cape Cod. I had been in the winter of my life when I first took his walks; and now, I could see, was spring, easing to summer.

I reread my "Mount Katahdin" section recently, and was startled by this line: *Would love to have the thoughts of the firs traded for my own. Snow / ice / sun.*

Had I made a wish, and had my Dutch friend turned it into a prophesy—a mortal turned into a tree? Factually, I had come down from the Norwegian Arctic after meeting my future wife. Had she rendered my anxious thoughts smoother, cleaner, more elemental, something you could call arboreal? And did seeing the gods mean something like leaving yourself behind, like shedding yourself for a new form, a silent form who consumes sunlight and lives slowly in a count of centuries? I'd be lucky to trade my small humanity not only for a look at the gods but also for its consequence: to be made to grow again every spring.

MARIGOLDS

Part Two

I find some advantage in describing the experience of a day on the day following. At this distance it is more ideal, like the landscape seen with the head inverted, or reflections in water.

—Henry David Thoreau, April 20, 1854

Southwest

Henry wrote in his essay "Walking," "When I go out of the house for a walk, uncertain as yet whither I will bend my steps, and submit myself to my instinct to decide for me, I find, strange and whimsical as it may seem, that I finally and inevitably settle southwest, toward some particular wood or meadow or deserted pasture or hill in that direction . . . The future lies that way to me, and the earth seems more unexhausted and richer on that side."

And so, on the Fourth of July of this pandemic year, in Massachusetts, I walked southwest from my home, where Jenny and I had gone to live for the summer and fall. This was the house where I grew up, vacated by my parents when they moved to the other side of the wide saltwater river that runs by our house. Our house is at the end of a peninsula, and the other shoreline—to the southwest—meets this side ten miles to the north, at the head of the river. Meaning, if I wanted to walk southwest like Henry, I'd have to start with an early morning swim.

I had coffee with Jenny, then packed a peanut butter and jelly sandwich, two chocolate chip cookies, a bottle of water, my phone, a twenty-dollar bill, a face mask, three pens, and two trash bags in my backpack. I said goodbye to Jenny, and in one of the most remarkably satisfying things I've done—so outdated that I'd never even thought to do it—I walked from my home toward a distant destination. Why haven't I done this before? I thought, striding across the lawn, turning to wave at Jenny one more time, and thinking of the miles that lay ahead of me. To put it another way: for the very first time in my life, I left home for the day without going out the driveway.

The route would take me along the southwest edge of Massachusetts and into Rhode Island, somewhere around sixteen miles to Sakonnet Point—another peninsula so isolated by the sea that it was a natural end to my day. But also, narratively neat, it was where my great-great-grandparents, from Chicago, summered.

Their son Demarest, my great-grandfather, eventually left Chicago for good, and bought the land where Jenny and I now lived. I was headed to the origin point of my family in New England. Unlike Henry, who walked southwest because "the future lies that way," I walked southwest to encounter the past.

A thousand feet from my front door, I walked past the dog cemetery, where a hundred years of my family's dogs had been buried under modest gravestones, and then down to the shoreline. I put my food, money, phone, and shoes in one of the trash bags, and walked into the water.

I never swam here, because I still thought of this stretch of water as the place where, over twenty years earlier, I'd seen a drowned girl. I had been fourteen, alone at home, when my aunt—who lived in another house on the peninsula—came running up from the shoreline, saying she'd heard screaming, and that two kids had just swum ashore saying their sister was lost in the water. I ran down the dock with my uncle, got in his boat. We looked down into the water for some time before a rescue diver waved at us. My uncle motored over. I stood at the boat's railing. Her body was clouded by the green water of midsummer. Her face fallen on the diver's shoulder. There was seaweed caught in her bathing suit. She looked to be my age, maybe a year or two older. The diver pushed her onto the boat, by my feet, then pulled himself up onto the deck. He tore off his mask and unclipped his oxygen tank and collapsed beside her, giving her CPR, until he stopped.

Halfway across the water now, all I could think about was the girl, how I didn't know anything about her, not even her name, but I knew her face, the seaweed in her bathing suit, how her slack arm had hit the boat's railing hard.

In the water, I must have swam past a jellyfish, because my armpit and chest felt combed by razors.

On the other side, I walked southwest, along the shoreline, near where my extended family collectively own land. To the south, clouds passed over an ocean holding lakes of sunlight under a northerly, autumn-like wind.

I followed the grassy road where frogs small as bumblebees appeared some rainy spring nights. Past the pond where I used to go duck hunting with my dad. Past the bushes of wild hazelnuts my mom and I picked when I was a boy—the memory of which so quietly imprinted itself in my mind that I had forgotten we'd done that until I walked past them one day, saw their frilled encasings drooping by the footpath, and thought of my mom. Past killdeer, song sparrows, willets, robins, chipping sparrows, least terns, black ducks. Walls of phragmites—the invasive reeds I can't get myself to dislike because of how they sway in the wind, the sound of fabric rushing across itself. Past the red-winged blackbirds within the phragmites, perched, light enough to bend but not break the thin rods. Past the east-facing oak tree crouched by a sand dune, so gnarled by salty wind that it is shorter than me but three times as long—a pendant unfurling over a century. The very tip of the oak had expressed a few feet of burgundy leaves in contrast to the coat of otherwise green ones sheened like car metal. Past skeletons in owl pellets and the smell of beach roses. To the beach where my grandmother, mother, and I all played as kids in our own times, the beach surrounding the farmland my great-grandfather bought in the early 1900s. The outgoing tide had left a trim of folded particulate—seaweed and flecks of stone—that looked like a line drawing of distant mountains.

I know this beach better than any strip of land. Up to my right, in the dunes, was where, when I was six or seven, I hid in the grass and watched two people having sex. Down at a little inlet was where, years ago, I sat watching my friend and his fiancée standing in the shallows on an August night, after dinner, kicking their feet to illuminate bioluminescence. And all along the beach, my grandmother went every morning to pick up trash that had washed ashore.

A beach changes. The dunes where I saw the couple having sex were reshaped, then obliterated in less than a day during Hurricane Bob in 1991. My friend and his fiancée broke off their engagement, and my friend recently described his grief as "cold chemicals" in his stomach. My grandmother passed away when I was in high school, and now her oldest son, my septuagenarian uncle, picks up beach trash in the morning.

Writing this now, I'm reminded of what Annie Dillard wrote about sand in *For the Time Being*—that beach sand is, in fact, not shoveled up from the ocean floor, as I had imagined. That it often comes from a place far away from the sea itself. That lichens, ice, and salt crystals chew up stones; that glaciers grind boulders to grains; and that the dried rocky powder is lifted by the wind, taken seaward. That the sand made from these inland mills—the featherlight ones, the mountain-shaping ones—is then carried

THE WIND-BENT OAK TREE

by freshwater, by rain, by streams, then rivers, and finally out to sea before being pressed back ashore by currents and waves. That the sand I was walking on could have come from a mountain a hundred miles away and started its journey many thousands of years ago. That, in fact, nothing is as simple as it seems, or, more, nothing is *at all* as it seems, and usually older. That this ground could have been carried by the wind before settling here.

I arrived at an inlet at the far end of the beach. I wrapped my journal and shoes in the trash bag, and walked into the sea for the second time that morning, hoping the jellyfish had been pushed offshore by the outgoing tide.

Hours later—after walking through salt marshes, down a long beach, and paying a guy to take me across an unswimmably wide harbor on his little motorboat—I found myself walking in a seaside community by the Rhode Island border, the kind with white picket fences and weatherworn shingles spread across large homes. Flagpoles spiking from hedged gardens. Clusters of hydrangeas bubbled around wraparound porches. Boxwoods lining brick pathways. Stopping across the street from a house that had its own tower and balcony, I saw a large family gathered on the lawn for this Fourth of July.

"The most tasteful front-yard fence was never an agreeable object of study to me," Henry wrote. "The most elaborate ornaments, acorn-tops, or what not, soon wearied and disgusted me. Bring your sills up to the very edge of the swamp."

Suddenly, the tinny sound of a marching band came from down the street, and a maroon van decorated in bunting and American flags careened around the corner. Two masked men were standing out the sunroof, waving American flags that they struggled to control in the wind. Bullhorns strapped to the roof blasted a frantic instrumental with a passionate horn section.

I sat on a wall so old that green and orange lichen covered nearly all the stones, and watched the van approach.

Were these men unaware of the violent undertones in being masked, waving a flag, from the roof of a van? One of the boys from the tower house ran toward the street, held up his hand, and hollered for America. "Two or three hours' walking will carry me to as strange a country as I expect ever to see," Henry once wrote.

THE FOURTH OF JULY

The van was gone as quickly as it had come, and I continued through the little community, passed through somebody's lawn, and went down to the shore, took a right, and started a long walk through alternating sections of private and public beaches. The private ones—whiter and sparser—were posted with large signs about keeping out without membership, but were exactly the same in sand and water as the public ones.

Before lunch, I walked past a small group of boys and one girl standing in a circle around a sandcastle, tossing in handfuls of sand. I overheard that they had caught a crab and put it in their castle.

"Should I throw a rock on it?" the tallest boy, likely the oldest, asked.

I turned, saw that he already held a large rock in his hand.

"Should I?" he said again, this time lifting the rock over the castle.

I kept walking.

"Bombs away!" I heard him yell.

Moments later, the little girl passed me, quietly running away from the group. Two other boys, smaller, the group's youngest, followed.

"Let's not talk about what we did today," one of the boys said as he passed me.

"I won't," the other said.

The boys speed-walked all the way to their family's blanket down the beach, maybe feeling for the first time the tension of temptation and thrill, of transgression or, maybe, power over something smaller and weaker. They'd killed something, or been a part of killing something. They didn't know how to explain the lingering discomfort to themselves except, as one of the boys suggested, to try to ignore the memory. These are not malicious boys, I thought then. Not rare in what they'd done. They were two common boys—two of many other boys who would stand over the crab, waiting to see the stone crush it. They would become two common young men, would witness predation in other ways—social or cultural or political— and would likely do nothing to stop it. But what of the taller one? The boy who had gone to find the rock, who had looked for one just big enough to smash the crab but small enough that he could carry it easily? The one who had asked the question with the rock already in his hand, planning to kill but needing the group to approve before he did it? Who would he become? What did he need?

I had killed minnows and crabs when I was a boy. These days, I don't like killing wasps or spiders or beetles, and when Jenny and I find a bug in the house, I get paper and a water glass, and scoop it up and take it outside. Jenny says it's endearing, but it's not only out of care. It's out of a debt of guilt for what, as a boy, I smashed. This past summer, I found myself running through the house, trying to catch a wasp the size of a baby carrot with a fishing net, afraid of its enormity but even more afraid of the responsibility of its death. We looked up the wasp online: it's called a cicada killer, grows nearly two inches long, and is known as the "gentle giant" of wasps. How would I have felt then, had I crushed a gentle giant? I've been repenting for the small animals for a very long time, I think.

Walking farther down the beach, I watched a girl searching for shells, curating her collection by holding each shell in her palm for some moments before deciding whether it would go in her bucket.

I stopped to eat my peanut butter and jelly sandwich on a dune at one of the private beaches. Toward the water, a woman was saying to her husband that she could, in fact, do a cartwheel. He said he didn't think so.

She was wearing a big pink floppy hat and shorts over her bathing suit. He was wearing nothing that looked like he was at the beach, but, rather, like he was at a golf tournament. She repeated that she could, yes, do a cartwheel. The man smiled, shook his head. She took off her hat, asked him to hold it. She put her feet together, gymnast-like, and held her hands at her side.

Her husband walked in front of her, waiting for her to—what? Fail? Succeed?

I had stopped eating my sandwich. Stared.

She then held her arms up, took another breath. She stepped, tilted toward the ground, and made one, very scrunched-up, cartwheel—legs buckled and body tilted. Still, she'd made it upside down and over. She stood up triumphantly, smiling.

I felt like clapping.

She snatched her hat back from her husband as if it were a prize, and then laughed.

"I did it!" she said.

He nodded, but said nothing more.

Not much happens along the beach for stretches of time, but if I lingered by people, I might witness compact dramas. Like a crab's death; a fledgling patriarchy. A cartwheel; a marriage story. Sometimes these

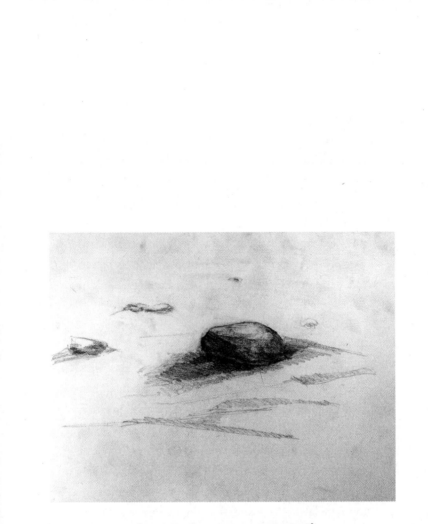

A STONE ON THE BEACH

dramas required no attention, no interpretation or expansion of meaning. Like, an hour or so after the cartwheel, I walked by half a dozen men playing beer pong on a plywood table in a parking lot. I watched one of them stare at a teenage girl walking by their game. He started humping the air. "I'd eat that ass!" he called loud enough for her to hear. He was hunched over the plywood table, pinching a weightless ball in one hand, looking at a cup of beer, hoping to sink it, which would, I assumed, make him feel good.

The stones changed in Rhode Island, which I noted because nothing else was different over the state line. The stones in the walls were darker and flatter than those in my hometown. There's a part of me that still expects more physicality in a border, as maps show. River borders and coastlines are nearly lyrical to cross—how, in them, nature eddies bureaucracy: a muddy river transitioning tax codes; tidal pools edging new laws. I've heard that the demilitarized zone between North and South Korea has some of the best bird-watching in the region, with a rare crane species that survives in the buffer of wilderness provided by a history of war. Wouldn't that be nice, if rare birds were living in every country's outline?

I had turned inland, to go along the roadways, in the final couple of hours of the walk, because the coastline appeared crenellated on my map, and I was afraid of running out of sunlight.

When you walk down a rural road, especially in the early summer, you might see sweetness in people: like a red ribbon tied around the wooden neck of a goose-shaped mailbox; gardens filled with sunflowers that are annuals, and so you know this homeowner took the time to plant something that will last only a year, that one season of a big yellow flower is enough. I'd never really gardened until this past spring, and wasn't surprised when it made me happy. But I was surprised by the surges of happiness, the levels of joy that come with, for instance, watering plants. It feels nearly a celebration to stand in a garden and aim a hose at a growing flower, watching spray arc through the air, helping the flower reach its colorful and reproductive peak. Or, later, to watch bumblebees socket themselves in the many vertical flower chambers of the foxgloves I planted—those cones of sherbet-colored bells. I was delighted the foxgloves survived, and that, in a way, I served a meal to bees. I have killed so many plants by mistake, watched them wither or wilt, denude. Or perhaps *killed* is the wrong word. I have let them go. I have not given them what they needed. My executions were of inaction, inability, and bad guesswork. Not enough water, or too much, sandier soil, shade too dense.

On the road, I walked past a man cleaning his mailbox in front of a wall with a hundred feet of roses.

I took a brief break under the shade of a catalpa tree adorned with cones of white flowers, and then continued walking, until, eight hours and sixteen miles after leaving my doorstep that morning, I sauntered into Sakonnet, where my great-great-grandparents had summered. The side of my right foot was burning and aching, and something in my knee was clicking. I am in my midthirties, I thought then. I used to be able to hike all day up and down mountains, and now flat, paved ground has become injurious.

I had been to Sakonnet Harbor once before.

This was about a decade ago, when I met my friend Ethan at his commercial fishing boat to motor offshore for a couple of hours and haul in dogfish at sunrise. Commercial fishing is not like fishing with a rod. It's not catching one fish at a time. You don't remove the hook and then decide to keep the fish or toss it back. You don't have the satisfaction that you are hunting, that this fish on your line has somehow chosen you just as you have somehow chosen it; that you have a relationship with the fish that will ultimately end in its death or in your pardon.

The dogfish came up in numbers, gasping and bleeding in the brightly colored nets that had been hung between buoys for a few days. The nets were hauled aboard by a winch—what looks a giant metal spool. As a net rose from the sea, Ethan and his first mate and I picked out the dogfish—each a couple of feet long—and tossed them in a plastic barrel. Rarely, a dogfish would slip by, too tangled, and then be crushed under the splitting weight of the net tightening around the winch. The winch would be stopped, reversed, and the broken fish would be untangled and added to the barrel.

I stared into the barrel after the first haul. The sharks' eyes were glassy blue-green. Some were blue like my dad's eyes. Others, celery colored. Obscenely beautiful, kitschy eyes, with pupils of coal-black that made the surrounding irises nearly shimmer. I looked closely at a shark on top of the pile—it had dots of silver or gold in its eye, as if washed with flecks of mica.

I've hunted ducks. I've fished. I've learned that animals look different up close, are endowed with

details and colors that you'd never see without holding them. The teal window on a mallard's wing is
more iridescent than it is through binoculars. The
purplish glow on a bluefish's side is as deeply glossed-
out as paint enamel. And then, here—I thought
the eyes of a dogfish were the prettiest eyes I'd ever
seen. Most people have duller eyes than these little
sharks that hunt the lightless seafloor. If you're an
omnivore, you might feel guilty at some point about

being the reason for an animal's death. You might be thinking of an animal's feelings, consciousness, or right to a natural death. But I think that guilt could come from a place far less abstract—a fleshier place that most omnivores don't see anymore: the body of an animal, and how beautiful it can be to almost all our senses. The warmth of a cow's neck on a cold day. A pig's eyelashes. The color of a dairy calf's nose. The softness of lamb's wool. When, throughout this summer, I call to my two chickens to roost, these birds come to my feet, look at me with tilted heads, and I see the depth of red in their combs as vibrant as blood in a Rembrandt painting. They coo when they hear my footfalls down the garden path in the morning. I see them standing at the fence when I round the corner, waiting for me to open the gate. How sweet their cooing is, and how sad it would be if it ended.

Ethan said the dogfish would be shipped off to England, for fish and chips.

"They used to use cod," he said as we motored back that afternoon, years ago.

"Do these taste like cod?" I said.

"They deep-fry them," he said. "It all tastes the same."

So, here I was, back in Sakonnet.

The gravel driveway to my ancestral summer home was edged with old cedars and flanked by hayfields. Through the hayfields was milkweed—their paddle-shaped leaves scooped upward—crowned with many butterflies. The house was on the knoll about a quarter mile down the driveway. I didn't know who owned the house now, only that it had been sold by my family sometime in the 1950s.

It's not very interesting to hear about another family's history. We all know this. Like dreams, family histories are self-centered and usually not stories—they are facts that you feel connected to, and that might endow your own life with an unearned sheen of greatness or bravery or whatever characteristic your ancestor lived up to. Nonetheless, with that disclaimer written, here are some tidbits, in generational order, that can add meaning to the house I was walking toward.

My great-great-great-grandfather founded a newspaper in the 1850s that merged with the *Chicago Tribune*,
and his daughter Jessie Bross married a young journalist
who worked at the *Tribune*: my great-great-grandfather
Henry Demarest Lloyd. It was Henry and Jessie who
summered in Sakonnet. Henry Demarest Lloyd was a
socialist, broke the story on Rockefeller's Standard Oil,
and, so says his Wikipedia entry, is credited as pioneering
muckraking journalism. He wrote a book called *Wealth
Against Commonwealth*, which I've tried to read over the
years but each time have been worn down by its ham-
mering, prosaic tone. It is a 536-page argument against
monopolies, to put it plainer than he'd ever wanted.

Jessie, his wife, also a socialist, opened their home
in Chicago as a refuge for victims of domestic abuse
and impoverished immigrants. We're all proud of Jessie. Their eldest son followed his parents' humanitarian,
socialist ideals, cofounded the Communist Labor Party
of America, and married the famous feminist, pacifist,
and suffragist Lola Maverick. The other son, Demarest, cashed out on his parents' inheritance and moved
east—because, my mother thinks, his parents were so
busy with work and social welfare programs that they
disregarded him, which made him resent them. Here
in Massachusetts, he apparently became an openly

adulterous, laudanum-addicted social ultraconserva-
tive who employed a Nazi-sympathizing housekeeper
and died of a drug overdose—in his bed and found by
his mistress—at his house in Potomac, Maryland, in
1937. This man was my great-grandfather. He was the
one who bought the peninsula where Jenny and I now
live, where my great-grandmother Katherine built a
dance hall that we've converted into our house.

I've never once thought that this house and land
that I inherited through my great-grandfather was
tainted, but I do imagine there was a lot of sadness
here, and sometimes I can see it inscribed right in the
land, other times tucked away in the houses. In ways
that are obvious, like the little family graveyard where
Demarest and Katharine's son's memorial shows his life
ending at twenty-four when his plane was shot down in
World War II. Or in an attic, where my mother found
blue-ribboned bundles of letters that Katharine saved
from the lovers—or crushes—she had before meeting
her husband. There is one letter from the son of the
Japanese ambassador to the United States, another
from the secretary of state who secretly made out with
her when she was only sixteen—*Burn this letter*, he'd
written on every letter she saved. But the most riveting
letters are from an Egyptologist who joined his father

in entering King Tutankhamun's tomb. *Dear Katinka*, he nicknamed her in his letters, and then described taking a felucca down the Nile at sunset.

I wondered if Katharine thought about the Egyptologist when she was here, at the house in Massachusetts, in the winter, when the snow fell against the windows and the dance hall was empty and her husband was in a laudanum stupor or off with his mistress. I imagined her standing at the window, staring out at a dull gray sky over a dull gray sea, perhaps watching a few brown sparrows sift through the defoliated rosebushes that her gardener tended in the summer. Did she think of her Egyptologist then? Of the sound of the Nile's water lapping against the felucca, the warm African sun on her skin, of him entertaining her with stories about breaking into tombs, about a civilization that thrived, then vanished, leaving behind enormous pyramidal monuments that were sky-scraping gravestones? Did she, in short, regret her decision to marry my great-grandfather, this man who discarded her for another woman?

The other day I was digging a deep hole in my garden and lifted a shovelful of dirt in which was what looked like a section of a drinking straw. I picked it out, blew off the dirt. It was clay, handmade, and with a wire-thin hole through the middle. On the ceramic fragment were two words: *Glasgow* on one side, and *Davidson* on the other. I knew from my college archaeology classes that I was holding part of an old smoking pipe. The cylindrical part of the pipe—the stem—which would get soggy in the mouth, break off, and then be spat to the ground. The fragment was easy to date because it had broken so perfectly on lettering that told it was manufactured sometime between 1861 and 1891.

I mention this because my great-grandmother's life, and maybe her sadness, seems fundamental to me. Seems like a bass note. But I'm reminded that there's always something older, that no human story is permanent. There was happiness and labor and a thousand other stories behind my great-grandparents' sorrow. There was a farmer standing in the place where my garden was, sometime around the Civil War, decades before Katharine was born. He was likely happy to be smoking his pipe. Perhaps it was after a long day of work, after he'd been shearing or planting. He might have been tired and sweaty, sat down in the grass to watch the sunset. Perhaps the war had just ended, and there was a general feeling of exhaustion rippling throughout New England. What did the ground feel like on his thighs? I wonder.

Katharine, and my thought of her standing in the living room looking out to the snow and the leafless rosebushes, would be far in this farmer's future. Beyond his death, even. The potential for Katharine to choose the Egyptologist, to float down the Nile, to not be cornered in a marriage, was still there. It was all potential for her.

It only got worse, in a way, for great-grandmother Katharine. After Demarest died, she allegedly married a closeted man whom she divorced when she found him having an affair with a man they both knew. And I recently discovered that things were maybe worse, or crueler, for Demarest than is recorded, too: My grandmother told my mom that she was convinced her father's mistress had murdered him. A teenager at the time, my grandmother was visiting the Potomac house when she heard him and his mistress yelling at each other through the night about a change he'd just made to his will. The next day, he was dead.

A last will and testament makes you stop dreaming, I think. You take stock of exactly what's around you at that moment, not what you hope will be around you. I was twenty-five when I wrote my first will, when I included this dance hall that my parents had already given to me. It made me think of the building more than I had before, of what I was inheriting. An empty dance hall is an invitation, somewhere between a plea and a hope.

I was thinking about young Demarest when I approached the Sakonnet home, how he was a boy once, how he and his family boarded a train in Chicago every year and rode east for days toward the coast, toward summer— the thought of which likely fermented a specific joy in him, the kind any kid feels traveling to a vacation at the beach. It would have been an overnight train. Maybe he had packed special snacks, or had chosen special toys. Was he a kind boy, who walked down to this beach to find seashells and rocks and add them to a collection he lined up on the windowsill of his bedroom? Or was he like that boy holding the stone over the trapped crab, asking others if he should drop it, already having decided to drop it? Did Katharine know when she met him that he was the type of boy who would hold the stone?

Signs reading Private Property and No Trespassing and warnings of surveillance were posted along the driveway, which I followed to the house, where there was a stone archway wide enough for a car, leading to what could only be called a courtyard.

I'd read that Jessie called their summer home the "house without a key" because anyone could drop in whenever, and that per my ancestors' socialist beliefs, they didn't have any servants, instead assigning guests

GATE AT THE END OF THE WALK

chores upon arrival. *Wealthy bohemians* might be an accurate depiction: I'm imagining lively dinner discussions about Karl Marx; a writer lying supine on wicker furniture beside an open seaside window, newspaper fluttering on his lap; empty teacups scattered across coffee tables. I later came across a picture of Jessie Bross and Henry Demarest Lloyd in Sakonnet, taken around 1895. She sits on a stone wall, in a black skirt, white jacket, and a fisherman's cap. She's breaking a smile, looking right at the photographer. Her husband is behind, legs up on the stone wall, in a full suit, wearing a tam-o'-shanter, his eyes deep in shadow.

I didn't see a doorbell beneath the archway. I didn't even see an obvious front door. I stood in the courtyard, timidly calling for someone. I took off my hat, ran my fingers through my tangled hair, salt-encrusted from the water crossings.

There were a few cars with Illinois license plates, as if my family had never left.

"Hello?" I called again, nervous now, looking up at the surrounding windows and wondering about Rhode Island's gun-ownership laws.

I was about to turn away when a man appeared on the other side of the courtyard, from behind one of the cars.

I smiled, waved, said I was sorry to barge in like this, but this had been my family's home a long time ago and would he mind if I just looked around?

He was young and sternly built, with a handsome cowlick and blue eyes. He looked at me as he walked across the courtyard.

"Ben?" he said.

"Yes?" I said, startled he knew my name.

"It's Brian."

I did know him, I saw then. He owned the farm down the street from which my family used to get Christmas trees.

"What are you doing here?" I asked.

"This is my family's house," he said.

I didn't understand. His farm was across the state line, in Massachusetts.

His family was from Chicago, he explained, and he and his dad had come here to look for property, and bought this land. He'd also bought a farm.

"But you live here?" I asked.

"Yeah."

He was polite, casual, had clearly not been struck by the same density of coincidence I was working through. He might have been wondering what I was doing at his house; I was trying to understand how it was possible that all these years I had known the person who lived on my great-great grandparents' plot.

He then explained that the house I was looking at was not the same house my great-great-grandparents had lived in. Only later did I read that the Lloyds' house had been sold to another family (not Brian's) in the mid-century, and then demolished in 1959, after the contents were auctioned off. That family then sold the land to Brian's family, and his family had built this house on the old plot. In all, it meant that I had not, really, walked to my ancestral home.

"I can show you around if you want," he said.

He took me to the front, to a green lawn that unfurled to the sea in the way that F. Scott Fitzgerald described in *The Great Gatsby*. His father emerged from the house, joined us. Then his niece, a college student also from Chicago, here for a vacation, walked out to the lawn.

"What are you doing?" Brian asked her.

"Just came out to see who this was," she said, about me.

"He just walked from Massachusetts," Brian said to her.

"What?" she said. "Why?"

I smiled, told her I was here to visit my ancestral home—but that, yes, I knew this wasn't really the same house.

"That's right," Brian's father said. Everything, even the landscaping, was different.

I suddenly felt foolish, making a pilgrimage to something that wasn't there anymore.

I turned to the sea quickly, and pointed to what remained the same.

"That's the view they must have had," I said.

"That's right," the father said.

The four of us stood on the lawn, looking out to the horizon. Three generations of a family, and me.

The father turned back to the house.

The niece scrolled through her phone.

"Well," Brian said. "Anything else you want to see? I can take you inside if you want."

I'd just be looking at someone else's house if I did that, and the absurdity of my walk would come into focus with a clarity that would embarrass me.

"No, thanks," I said.

"Okay," Brian said. "You want a ride down the driveway?"

"No thanks," I said.

"You sure?" he said.

SAKONNET, BEACH AND LIGHTHOUSE

"I'm sure," I said.

I turned back toward the house, and then saw a large granite hummock behind it.

"That rock," I said to Brian and his dad, for the niece had already wandered back into the house. "I recognize that rock from an old picture."

"That's right," the father said. "It's always been there."

I walked closer to the rock, and noticed then that an infinity pool had been built into the side of it. I felt nothing, no connection to my family, staring at the clear pool water backed into stone that had been made four billion years earlier.

"We must know the right before we can do the right," my great-great-grandfather wrote in *Wealth Against Commonwealth*. "The first step to a remedy is that the people care. If they know, they will care."

I stood halfway down the driveway, looking at the monarch butterflies in the field. Someone shot off an early firework. I kept forgetting that today was a celebration of America. We were in the middle of a pandemic. In a few months, the death toll from the virus in America would reach a quarter million people. The president, on national television, would continue to refuse to disavow white supremacists. Millions believed that some Democrats were pedophilic vampires, and some of those same people would eventually attack the Capitol. I lived in a country with the most expensive military in the world but without a plan for climate change.

"To help them to know and care," Henry Demarest Lloyd continued, "to stimulate new hatred of evil, new love of the good, new sympathy for the victims of power, and, by enlarging its science, to quicken the old into a new conscience, this compilation of fact has been made."

Wealth Against Commonwealth was published in the 1890s—before World War I, before World War II, before the atomic bomb and the effects of DDT and Tuskegee and Vietnam, before so much that governments and companies had done or covered up to hurt or kill. Perhaps there was still some hope left, then, in the 1890s, that if only the higher powers got the facts, they would enact goodness. That in the first steps into an industrialized nation, there was still room to be hopeful about individual rights.

"Democracy is not a lie," he wrote as one of the last lines of his book, as if a wish and a fact.

What was it I'd heard about monarch butterflies? I thought, standing in the field. That they were dying out because of habitat loss? Or air pollution? Or monoculture? Or climate change? Or invasive species? I couldn't remember exactly why, but was sure it was people who had done it.

"We should go forth on the shortest walk, perchance," Henry wrote in "Walking," "in the spirit of undying adventure, never to return,—prepared to send back our embalmed hearts only as relics to our desolate kingdoms."

I didn't want to send back my embalmed heart. I returned home that night gladly and fully, by sunset, wanting a shower and to lie down. Jenny had planned to pick me up in Sakonnet, but just as she was getting in the car, our dog ran after a deer, into the woods and through a marsh. Jenny had followed, into the woods, through the marsh, calling our dog, Sally's, name, and so she couldn't leave the house. My mom—who lives just fifteen minutes down the road—offered to pick me up instead. Sally had come home on her own, when the deer outran her.

That evening, Jenny and I watched sunken clouds drift over the marsh and under a swatch of herringbone clouds gripping the high sky. Some distant wind and pressure had shaped an anvil of a cloud tipping north and lit with a molten trim. I will never get tired of looking at the clouds in sunlight. What useless overstuffed beauty, the clouds. How overly abundant. Would it be more practical, more efficient in nature, if evaporated water hung fog-like, if the sky were the steamy room between the ground and atmosphere? But, here is the earth we have: bodily sunlit masses, deckled scraps of feathered and air-lifted water.

"I think that I cannot preserve my health and spirits," Henry wrote, "unless I spend four hours a day at least—and it is commonly more than that— sauntering through the woods and over the hills and fields, absolutely free from all worldly engagements."

I had walked nine hours and sixteen miles that day, but I didn't feel healthier or in higher spirits, exactly. I didn't need the walk in the same way I had needed Cape Cod, years earlier, when walking down a beach was like hungering for a mineral missing from my bloodstream. What I had now were the images of the day. I had the sunlight on the sea in the morning. I had my pausing beside the oak tree, trying to name the new leaves' particular shade of green until I realized they were not green at all, but burgundy. Boys with a crab. An infinity pool cupped to a prehistoric rock. No spiritual or healthful imperative as Henry might have gotten—only everyday humanity crossing my path, on the way to a family home that wasn't even there.

There's a paragraph in "Walking" that lends itself easily to the metaphor we make of walking: "What is it that makes it so hard sometimes to determine whither we will walk? I believe that there is a subtle magnetism in Nature, which, if we unconsciously yield to it, will direct us aright. It is not indifferent to us which way we walk. There is a right way; but we are very liable from heedlessness and stupidity to take the wrong one. We would fain take that walk, never yet taken by us through this actual world, which is perfectly symbolical of the path which we love to travel in the interior and ideal world; and sometimes, no doubt, we find it difficult to choose our direction, because it does not yet exist distinctly in our idea."

In walking, as in living, you must choose a path. You must go one way, and so give up another way. I had just walked to my ancestors' summer home, and so had wondered about their paths with the clarity of hindsight. Like, did my great-grandmother feel that she chose the wrong path by marrying a man who would succumb to addiction and cheat on her? Did my great-great-parents feel like they'd chosen the right one, the socially benevolent one, at the expense of perhaps not giving their younger son the love he needed? Are we bound to turn down the wrong paths in our lives, stalked by bad luck or misfortune? How, in short, do we turn ourselves to the southwest of our lives?

After dinner, Jenny and I walked down to our dock. I saw violet-blue platelets of gasoline on the water in the marsh, no larger than hands, catching in the grass.

CLOUDS OVER SALT MARSH

Interlude III

Years ago, in January, before my Cape Cod walk, I was carrying a wooden boat across icy ground, slipped, and the boat's gunwale came down on my hands. A half inch of my middle finger lay in the dead grass. I wish I could accurately describe the feeling of picking up the fingertip—how immediately protective I was, holding it in my palm, cupping it like I'd found a bird's egg; how I felt it was both numb and not numb because it was then an object, not part of my body anymore. It was of my left hand—my writing and painting hand. "We have to go," I said to my friend John, who carried the other side of the boat.

The surgeon couldn't sew it back on, so I was sent home with lots of drugs, and later returned to the hospital for a skin graft, to cap off the fingertip. Before the operation, the surgeon said that if he couldn't graft the skin from the lower part of the finger, he'd bend the finger and attach the open end to my palm, that the skin would grow from palm to fingertip, and then he'd cleave it free later. He wouldn't know if he needed to do that until I was under anesthetic, he said. I woke up to my finger not sewed to my palm, but with a bulb of bandages and an aluminum plate shoved under the nail bed.

I dreamt for weeks that animals were chewing my fingers. I woke up one night sure that someone was holding my hand. Pain arrived in the most creative ways: buzzing that felt like sound, pinches, bites, whirs, reenactments of the amputation, pins and needles, burning as if my finger were in a candle flame. Mostly, the stub on my fingertip felt as if it were being hit lightly by a small hammer all day. When I called the nurse to ask if the pain was normal, she said, "Your fingertip was exploded off."

In the week I'd lost my fingertip were some of the coldest days in Massachusetts since 1918, which is why the ground was so slippery. A few days before I was carrying the boat, Mount Washington, one hundred and fifty or so miles to the north, tied with a small town in Canada for the second coldest place on earth, with a wind chill of negative eighty. Mattresses of sea ice floated into the river outside my house. The high tide left waxy skirts of ice up on the dock pilings. The overwintering birds quieted down. I watched a fox walk across a stretch of water I hadn't seen freeze since I was in grade school.

My house was too cold. I was anxious with pain post-surgery. The wood floors stung my feet when I got out of bed. So I moved into my parents' house, a quarter mile across the bay—partly because of the cold, mostly because I couldn't wash the dishes or drive a car or cut an onion or open a jar of peanut butter.

My mind was too soft with pain and painkillers for reading, and with no internet or usable cell service at my parents' house—surrounded by old farm fields, way out on a broad peninsula—I'd turn on the television and watch the evening news. An ecstatic weatherman ranted about the cold snap. Like the sky had broken, a stick bent too far by the hands of winter. The weatherman pointed to a long blue necklace of temperature low points slung through the next dozen January days: Sixteen degrees. Fourteen. Twenty-one, eleven, twenty-three. He nearly yelled, rapturous, delivering the bad news everyone already felt pressing in all around them.

To stave off cabin fever, I made it my daily task to find the snowy owl that had recently arrived on the moors. She was most often on the ground, on a hummock, her white body luminescing. There's no bird so mammalian as a snowy owl: coal-black eyes, hunched over, tall as a baby. I shouldn't have followed her from the moors to the beach to the marsh. To be outside in this hundred-year freeze. Inevitably, my finger nub would throb—maybe the metal plate had chilled to some unforgiving temperature. I'd stick the finger in my mouth, breathe through the bandages, track home, light the stove, and hold my hand over the flame until the pain softened.

After failing to enjoy almost any part of television and without the attention span for novels, I picked up the book my dad had given me for Christmas: Henry David Thoreau's *The Journal 1837–1861*, edited by Damion Searls. I had been resisting it because I remembered Thoreau—from my high school reading of him—as a boring, misanthropic writer who'd lived beside his mother and grew beans as if he were Aristotle.

I turned to his winter entries to see how he might better describe these weeks that I was finding more and more painful to endure. "The surface of the snow in the fields is that of pretty large waves on a sea over which a summer breeze is sweeping," he wrote on January 22, 1852—also a description of the snowfields spread out in front of my parents' house. I came across passage after passage of poetic, oddly familiar writing, and suddenly felt a kinship to this observer.

"Is not January the hardest month to get through?" he wrote one day, over a century and a half ago. Yes, I thought. It is. I agree with you so much, I thought.

And so, this became my habit for the historic cold month: look for the snowy owl, light a fire at home, read a few journal entries. Watch the fire break into itself. Fall asleep under the vague effects of oxycodone. Wake and read another few journal entries.

Little did I know what awaited me: somewhere in the wintry soil was a tick larva that would, sometime in May, crawl up into the grass, cling to a rodent, bury its body in, sip Lyme spirochete, and then later fall off, hook to me, and flush the spirochete into my blood.

I had underestimated the scope of loss—half an inch isn't so big, really, on the body. But grief generates more than you started with, I've since learned. Sometimes I'd unwrap the bandages to look at what used to be my fingertip and was now a bloodless sore, skin sandpapered down. I learned that the tiny white crescent that remained of my nail was called a *lunula*, a "little moon." Two lines of stitches dovetailed across the tip. What an uneasy feeling to be repulsed by a part of myself I used to love, for who doesn't love their hands—the most astounding and used tools on your body. I found myself looking up anatomical illustrations of hands, noticing how many pieces were therein, how many small muscles in spindly bones, as compactly complicated as a small animal's skeleton. Yes, maybe that was it—that I hadn't realized hands were to me like independent creatures on my body, until one of them had been maimed.

Depression isn't the word for that January. It was more a thinning, a shortening of spirit. Henry put it better in his winter of 1842: "My soul and body have tottered along together of late, tripping and hindering one another." Why was it so comforting to read this antique account of winter and loss? Perhaps to acknowledge the immortality of weather. It was the weather report that the man on the evening news couldn't give: an interpretation of the effect negative numbers have on the skin and soul and home. Henry wrote in 1855: "Our thermometer stands at -14° at 9 AM; others, we hear, at 6 AM stood at -18°, at Gorham, N.H., -30°.

There are no loiterers in the street, and the wheels of wood wagons squeak as they have not for a long time,—actually shriek. Frostwork keeps its place on the window within three feet of the stove *all day* in my chamber . . . I was walking at five, and found it stinging cold. It stung the face." And the next day: "The coldest night for a long, long time was last . . . People dreaded to go to bed. The ground cracked in the night as if a powder-mill had blown up, and the timbers of the house also . . . Must leave many buttons unbuttoned, owing to numb fingers. Iron was like fire in the hands . . . The cold has stopped the clock . . . Bread, meat, milk, cheese, etc., etc., all frozen . . . The latches are white with frost and every nail-head in entries, etc., has a white cap . . . This, i.e. yesterday, the 6th, will be remembered as the cold Tuesday."

The temperature kept dropping that winter. The language of cold is a language of violence—*gripping, snapping, pinching, numbing*. The fear of falling temperatures is manifest in the way *cold* resists being a verb: while days in spring continue to *warm*, in summer to *heat up*, and in fall to *cool down*, what do they do in these painful winter months, in this downward swoop? *Freeze* isn't the word, as *freeze* implies some end point. *Cold* must stay an adjective, padded with verbs, a line of separation: the days *are getting colder*. When a friend from Sierra Leone called, I said, "The days here are still"—I paused—"coldening."

You can be imprisoned by it, or you can do as Henry did—put on a pair of skates and marvel at the hats of frost on the nailheads. At the end of January 1854, he wrote this homage to cold: "Last night I felt it stinging cold as I came up the street at 9 o'clock; it bit my ears and face, but the stars shone all the brighter. The windows are all closed up with frost, as if they were ground glass. The winter, cold and bound out as it is, is thrown to us like a bone to a famishing dog, and we are expected to get the marrow out of it . . . It is true it is like a cow that is dry, and our fingers are numb, and there is none to wake us up. But the winter was not given to us for no purpose. We must thaw its cold with our genialness. If it is a cold and hard season, its fruit, no doubt, is the more concentrated and nutty . . . I knew a crazy man who walked into an empty pulpit one Sunday and, taking up a hymn-book, remarked: 'We have had a good fall for getting in corn and potatoes. Let us sing Winter.' So, I say, 'Let us sing winter.' What else can we sing, and our voices be in harmony with the season?"

February came.

Cuts leave scars. Amputations leave nothing, only the air above them, a frightful new bit of air. My fingertip was a weird shape that did not resemble what it once was—the distinct form of a fingertip. Each one is like a tiny hull, a bow of a ship planked in ridges. The planking of my left middle fingerprint was now smudged with scars and grafted skin and somehow turned inside out, as if stirred through the middle and frozen into an eddy.

The left finger used to be longer by—how much? I drew one-sixteenth-inch marks on my right middle finger, held the left finger against it. Exactly seven-sixteenths of an inch shorter. In the days that followed, I couldn't help but notice other near-half inches: the width of a chocolate bar, a pill, a stack of pennies, Denis Johnson's *Train Dreams*.

That spring, at a dinner party, I was seated beside a German woman. She pointed to the bandage and asked what had happened. I told her about the boat. The slippery ground. The stitches. The metal plate. How I needed to wrap my fingertip against the cold because it felt permanently sunburnt, nerves destroyed and numbed.

She shrugged. She said I could have lost all my fingers.

"Glück im Unglück," she said. "In bad luck there is luck."

I agreed.

In bad luck, there is luck.

I could have said it another way: "Let us sing winter. What else can we sing, and our voices be in harmony with the season?"

Months after that, I ordered Thoreau's *Cape Cod*, and read a little passage every night before going to sleep.

The Allagash: *Nature Must Have Made a Thousand Revelations*

Last year I read a book on wildflowers that explained an easily overlooked truth: flowers that bloom at night are mostly white. Over millennia, darkness has deconstructed them to their foundations, lifting their contrast out of color entirely. They are also often intensely fragrant, making strong rivers of perfume that lead night-blinded pollinators to their pale sources. The fact reminded me of when I lived in San Francisco, where, walking home at night, after my internship at a publishing house, I'd pass through jasmine scent long before I saw the flowers. The smell strengthened as I walked a street block, eventually seeing white stars of flowers spilling over a garden fence or wrapped around telephone poles.

I was in my midtwenties then, an age when, as Henry wrote of his own midtwenties, "Our doubts are so musical that they persuade themselves." I had no idea what I wanted to do with my life, no obligations at home, nothing to get back to at the end of the day. So I always took the long way back to my apartment: looped through the Mission, up Noe Valley, inevitably passing more jasmine. I still remember one plant specifically, across from an elementary school, that overhung the sidewalk with flowers that you couldn't avoid walking straight through. Is this what the nocturnal pollinators like the moths felt, secreting along their paths, flower to flower? A kind of joy in unaccountability?

This was also when I met John, the one who was holding the other side of the boat when I slipped, and who later invited me to Norway. He worked at the publishing house. He lived on his uncle's boat. He took showers at the marina. He was thrashing into adulthood, like me. I started calling him my best friend a few weeks after we met.

Now, a decade later, John was married to Rebecca, living in a nineteenth-century farmhouse in a New Hampshire hill town. They had chickens and a dog and a vegetable garden, and were expecting their first baby. He had arrived at adulthood with all its ballasts, all its irreversible stability and decorations.

When I mentioned to him on the phone that I was reading about Henry David Thoreau's Maine journeys, and that I was thinking of following one, he said he'd be interested in joining. I called him back on a summer morning to ask if he felt like canoeing part of the Allagash, to reach the northernmost edge of Henry's 1857 Maine walk: a place called Pillsbury Island in the middle of a giant lake, where Henry—with his friend Ed and their Penobscot guide, Joe Polis—had stopped to take shelter during a thunderstorm.

"It will be a trip to the edge," I said to John. "The edge of Thoreau's walks. The edge of your life before fatherhood."

He said he'd bring his canoe, and that I should come up as soon as possible.

Jenny and I arrived at John and Rebecca's home in the early evening. We all swam in a nearby lake, drank beer on their lawn—beside old apple trees, and accompanied by the song of a nearby wood thrush—and then had a pasta dinner with salad greens John had picked from his garden. After dinner, I went outside to get my toothbrush from the car, and saw that the field in front of their house was filled with fireflies. "The fireflies appear to be flying," Henry wrote on a night like this

THE FIELD WHERE FIREFLIES GATHERED

one, 168 years ago. "Their light is singularly bright and glowing to proceed from a living creature." I listened to Jenny and our friends talking inside. Holding my toothbrush, I walked to the edge of the field and stared, letting the image of living sparks and the smell of the field and the sound of my family and friends at my back become a memory I would never forget.

The next morning, John and I tied his canoe to the roof of his truck, and then drove nine hours north—north until the roads lost their pavement, through long flat plains of pine swamps on either side of the road, within sixty miles of the Canadian border. We slowed at an entry posted with signs welcoming us to the Allagash Wilderness Waterway and asking that we please stop to register at the checkpoint. We stopped. I looked up, and saw the park attendant—blond wavy hair, wearing a Patriots jersey modified with a moose head—standing on the porch of the checkpoint, smoking. She lightly snuffed her cigarette when she saw us pull up, and then placed it in an ashtray for later.

We met her inside.

She offered us a donut from the twenty-four pack on her desk.

"The loggers brought them for me this morning," she said as she gathered the paperwork for us to complete.

"No, thanks," I said.

A guitar solo on the radio cut through the small ranger station. Packets of Oreos and bug spray were for sale beneath the radio. I looked through the window at the empty and dusty parking lot, at the dust-covered evergreens lining the empty road.

"Must not be many people going camping these days," I said. "With the pandemic."

"Tons," she said. "Busiest season we've had. Everyone wants to get the hell out of the cities."

I nodded, walked over to the rack of snacks and supplies. I picked out a slender bottle of organic bug spray.

"You're going to want the bigger one," she said over my shoulder. She pointed down the shelf, to a can as big as a Reddi-wip canister with the words *25% BONUS!* and *25% DEET* written over a graphic forest.

"I'm going for three days," I said, smiling, holding up the can, like, *This is crazy huge, right?*

"Well, that's the biggest we got," she said. "Don't worry, that'll be enough. That all?"

She rang me up for $123 for two nights' camping. Camping for which we had brought our own food, tent, canoe, and vehicle. I asked her to repeat the number.

I then held out a credit card.

"We don't take cards," she said.

"You don't?" I said.

"There's an ATM back in town," she said.

"Town?" I said. We hadn't passed through any towns.

"Millinocket."

"Is that far?"

"About an hour and a half back south," she said.

"An hour and a half back?" I said.

In my silence, I wondered who carried over a hundred dollars in cash when they went camping, and how many people took a three-hour detour to pay it.

John said he had a checkbook in the car.

"Who carries a checkbook in their car?" I asked him.

"A lot of places in New Hampshire don't take credit cards," he said.

"We do take personal checks," she said, smiling at John.

Allagash means "hemlock bark," Henry wrote, which in America smells of animal urine and in Europe is a famous poison (and a different type of tree). He went there, to the Allagash, because it contained places where you might, as he wrote, "live and die and never hear of the United States." In reality, the many loggers and hunters who lived along the Allagash Wilderness Waterway in the nineteenth century had certainly heard of the United States. In fact, before Henry got there, the loggers had *reversed* the direction of the hundred-mile-long river, from north flowing to south flowing, to avoid paying Canadian (British) taxes for the timber floating into the Canadian border. Perhaps they were more aware of America and its limits than anyone in the cities Henry was trying to avoid.

I had first read Henry's *The Maine Woods* in college, in a class on nature writing. There was one specific detail that had stuck with me, and I was happy to find it when I reread the book while planning this trip. It happens in the middle of the night, when Henry gets up and steps away from the campsite, presumably to pee. Alone, he's startled to see a glowing ring at his feet. It was "a perfectly regular elliptical ring of light, about five inches in its shortest diameter, six or seven in its longer, and from one eighth to one quarter of an inch wide. It was fully as bright as the fire, but not reddish or scarlet, like a coal, but a white and slumbering light, like the glow-worm's. I could tell it from the fire only

by its whiteness." What happens next is worth reading
in full:

I saw at once that it must be phosphorescent
wood, which I had so often heard of, but never
chanced to see. Putting my finger on it, with a
little hesitation, I found that it was a piece of
dead moose-wood (*Acer striatum*) which [Joe
Polis] had cut off in a slanting direction the
evening before. Using my knife, I discovered
that the light proceeded from that portion of
the sap-wood immediately under the bark,
and thus presented a regular ring at the end,
which, indeed, appeared raised above the level
of the wood, and when I pared off the bark
and cut into the sap, it was all aglow along
the log. I was surprised to find the wood quite
hard and apparently sound, though probably
decay had commenced in the sap, and I cut
out some little triangular chips, and, placing
them in the hollow of my hand, carried them
into the camp, waked my companion, and
showed them to him. They lit up the inside of
my hand, revealing the lines and wrinkles, and
appearing exactly like coals of fire raised to a

white heat, and I saw at once how, probably, the Indian jugglers had imposed on their people and on travelers, pretending to hold coals of fire in their mouths.

. . . It could hardly have thrilled me more if it had taken the form of letters, or of the human face.

I carried that image of Henry holding a white, glowworm-colored wood chip in his hand for years, and it is the one fact I repeated whenever I got in a discussion about his writing. It lends itself so smoothly to metaphor and meaning: a man carrying back to camp illuminated wood is, in a way, the heart of his work. *Look at this!* I felt him saying to me in his journals. *Look how strange!* The temptation is to think that if you spend enough time in the forest, you, too, might find something as extraordinary.

After the checkpoint, John and I took a wrong turn, stopped to watch two moose and a black bear on the road leading us in the wrong direction, and so were very late arriving at a stream that fed into the lake surrounding Pillsbury Island. But it was summer in the far north; twilight held two hours before midnight.

We lifted the canoe off the truck, put in our bags and food and paddles, and walked everything into the stream. The water, warm as dishwater, went up to our calves, and felt therapeutic after being in a car for so long. The river was too shallow to paddle, so we walked beside the floating canoe until we reached the lake.

Evergreens and foliage with the density of a rain forest lined the stream like curtains. The overhead sunset seemed to be lying and slipping upon the water. Mossy and grassy clearings and the overhanging oak and pine boughs gave me the impression of walking through a stage forest, an example of a forest—how deliberately the stream led us. "It was impossible for us to discern [the] trail in the elastic moss," Henry wrote about his journey near here, "which, like a thick carpet, covered every rock and fallen tree, as well as the earth."

Down the stream, I saw a frog, big as two clasped hands, on a stone. We stopped the canoe, and both pointed to the frog. It was facing upstream, and though we stood only a foot or two from it, the frog held its position, glistening under the twilight.

"Looks like a sentinel," John said. "A bullfrog, you think?"

I said I didn't know my frogs, but that was the biggest frog I'd ever seen.

It's hard not to feel special when a wild animal lets you gawk. The animal might be seeing *you*, not as a generally hazardous human, but as an individual. *I trust you not to do anything bad*, the frog's stillness at my feet could say. *And so, I'll sit within a step of you. Sure, my body—smaller than your foot—and bones— no thicker than the pencil in your journal—could be crushed. You might be carrying a stone, but I'd guess not.* Maybe what I want when I go out in nature is not to see it, but to be seen by it. To receive anointment.

We eventually exited the forest-stream-tunnel into the vast openness of the lake, sat in the canoe, and paddled north toward Pillsbury Island. "It was very exhilarating, and the perfection of traveling," Henry wrote, of his first moments stepping from land into a canoe, which he took down a river. "The coasting down this inclined mirror, which was now and then gently winding, down a mountain, indeed, between two evergreen forests, edged with lofty dead white pines, sometimes slanted half-way over the stream, and destined soon to bridge it."

We coasted on the water, under metallically blue twilight. Somewhere the lake floor was 124 feet below us, and right then, the water was draining of color, turning black. The quiet around us was made sharper

BULLFROG ON RIVER PATH

by our paddling, by the clucking lap of the water re-sounding through the body of the canoe.

"We heard an ox sneeze in its wild pasture across the river," Henry wrote of the silence around here.

I strained to see the island behind the coming dark, knowing only that it was north, tucked behind one of the many hemlock hummocks protruding from the lakeside. We canoed for an hour, until the atmosphere lost its tone of blue light and, like glass cooling, became translucent enough to show the stars behind it.

Eagle Lake was first famous for being the northern-most edge of Henry's Maine journey; then for being the site of an alien abduction.

It was August 1976. Four friends—art students from Boston—had traveled to the Allagash for a few days' fishing. On their first night camping, they saw a glowing orb over the trees on the horizon. It pulsed with colors before disappearing. Other people in the area later confirmed they also saw a strange light hovering above the trees. Nobody knew what it was.

The next night, the friends lit a bonfire onshore, then launched their canoe into Eagle Lake for night fishing. The pulsing light appeared again, but this time it was at the edge of the lake, much closer to them.

"I was in the back of the canoe and I noticed it first," one of the men later recalled on *The Joan Rivers Show*, after their story had become somewhat famous. "I felt like someone was staring at me . . . I turned around to look over my right shoulder, and there was a ball of light." He later made a sketch—like a droplet of magma in the night sky. "It looked very liquid in appearance, and the color changes went from red to green to bright yellow-white." It was as big as a two-story building and perfectly spherical. "You're literally awed by this sight," one of the others said. They had stopped paddling, were together staring at the light suspended over the treetops. Then it started moving toward them, over the lake. A spotlight hit the water, they said, and sped toward them. They tried to out-paddle the spotlight, but couldn't. The next thing they remember was that they were somehow back onshore, near their campsite, as if they'd just awoken there. They looked up, and saw the ball of light one last time. "Within seconds," one said, "this thing had gone up, and became a star. It moved around to the southwest on the horizon, and then just disappeared out of sight."

How did they land the canoe? they wondered as they sat there onshore. When they walked up to their campfire, they saw that it had burnt down to embers, as if many hours had passed. Hadn't they been out for a much shorter time? they thought. Twelve years later, after each underwent hypnotic regressions, their answers came: as if Joan Rivers said when she introduced the men on her show, in the time between the spotlight hitting the water and them being back onshore, "they'd actually been aboard the spacecraft, and had been subjected to a series of physical experimentations by alien beings." They'd been naked, on their backs, and couldn't move their limbs, they said. The aliens—four-fingered, with large, oval eyes—touched them, explored their bodies. "I remember they were doing something to my penis with some sort of device," one said to Joan. "I was feeling violated," another said.

Years passed, and one of the four said that while they did see strange lights, the abduction part was invented. He also said they were on drugs: "I remember Jack brought some Afghan temple ball with him to share with the rest of us . . . Yeah, we were definitely stoned when we went out on the lake just before we got that sighting." (The other three deny taking drugs.)

It's hard to believe the story as they tell it, but there's a stranger truth within the sighting, which might be noticeable only to a Henry David Thoreau reader: Henry also described unexplained lights hovering over the Allagash.

"The next day," Henry wrote, after telling his companions about the ring of phosphorescence, "[Joe] told me their name for this light,—*artoosoqu'*,—and on my inquiring concerning the will-o'-the-wisp, and the like phenomena, he said that his 'folks' sometimes saw fires passing along at various heights, even as high as the trees, and making a noise. I was prepared after this to hear of the most startling and unimagined phenomena, witnessed by 'his folks;' they are abroad at all hours and seasons in scenes so unfrequented by white men. Nature must have made a thousand revelations to them which are still secrets to us."

Could the friends have seen a massive will-o'-the-wisp—that rare phenomenon of energized blue or red or green light hovering over land? Did they mistake "fires passing along at various heights, even as high as the trees, and making a noise" for a spacecraft? Or was it the other way around? That the hovering fires, as told to Henry, were, in fact, spacecrafts so far beyond nineteenth-century technology that they could only be described as floating flames? I went looking for firsthand Penobscot accounts of something like what Henry described, and found a book published in

1893 by Joseph Nicolar, a Penobscot scholar from Old Town, Maine, where Joe Polis also lived. In his book, Nicolar told an origin story of people witnessing a fight between a shape-shifting loon (woman) and a swan. The people stood upon a mountain and "beheld the same white loon coming from the north very swiftly, and when it reached the place opposite where the dead swan lay, it made its usual circles, there it stood very high and very still for a few moments, then it turned itself into a great ball of fire, and fell swiftly down to the water; and when it struck the water, the earth shook and the roar of it was great." Nicolar also wrote this of the first man coming to Earth: "Unto the night the clouds carried me, and unto the darkness I was carried and in the midst of the darkness a voice spoke unto me, saying, 'even in the darkness I will be with thee.' These words brought light into the clouds so that the clouds which carried me was like a ball of fire, and the ball of fire gave us light while passing the darkness of the night, and when the darkness of the night passed toward the setting of the sun, the light of the day came from the rising of the sun.—And the clouds turned white and the brightness of fire was not there."

Perhaps the indigenous people in Maine watched some visitor from the edge of the galaxy hovering over

old-growth pine trees far before the loggers or Henry
David Thoreau ever got there. There are otherworldly
tones in Nicolar's fiery cloud drifting through the night
air and carrying a person, spacecraft-like, and in a fireball falling from the sky. But perhaps the likeliest and
most tragic misunderstanding is this: that four friends
on a weekend fishing trip were the lucky witnesses to
an "unimagined" phenomenon, that nature had given
a "revelation" to them, had given them one of the rar-
est natural sightings on our earth, which they couldn't
see because of the Afghan temple ball and the fact that
they lived after the moon landing.

"I let science slide," wrote Henry of his bioluminescent wood, "and rejoiced in that light as if it had
been a fellow creature. I saw that it was excellent, and
was very glad to know that it was so cheap. A scientific explanation, as it is called, would have been
altogether out of place there. That is for pale daylight.
Science with its retorts would have put me to sleep; it
was the opportunity to be ignorant that I improved.
It suggested to me that there was something to be seen
if one had eyes. It made a believer of me more than
before. I believed that the woods were not tenantless,
but choke-full of honest spirits as good as myself any
day,—not an empty chamber, in which chemistry was

left to work alone, but an inhabited house,—and for a few moments I enjoyed fellowship with them."

Is that what the four friends were saying, too? That for a few moments they enjoyed fellowship with something beyond humanity? When we reach the end of wilderness as humanity has known it for so long, when we come to the other side of the Industrial Revolution, railroads, deforestation, and the automobile, when there aren't many more places that we can call unknown, what do we do? Part of being a human is believing against the absence of proof that there is something beyond our view: a next life, divinity, monsters or sea serpents, a cultural utopia. While I'm not sure that heaven or hell or reincarnation exist as the common visions we associate with them, I'm positive that we need—or are always trying to reach—an unprovable yet *physical space* filled with phenomena that are definitively unearthly. For a long time, wilderness could fill that space—European Americans in the nineteenth century suggested there were woolly mammoths still grazing in the American West; there was the fairy craze in Victorian England. But when that wilderness has been recorded, photographed, and documented, perhaps, when you're in the middle of one of the most remote forests in Maine, there's only one option to satisfy that human need for the unknown, for that space beyond ourselves: looking up. To be abducted by aliens in 1976 might be the same as being taken by the grandeur of the wilderness in 1857. They are rivers of the same source: to be away from people, to be elevated from this world. For Henry, he wanted to be swept away from cities. For the Allagash Four, it was the earth itself.

"Now at length I was glad to make acquaintance with the light that dwells in rotten wood," Henry wrote of the bioluminescence that he had found that night. "I kept those little chips and wet them again the next night, but they emitted no light." What to do with something that seems impossible, beyond the edge of normalcy, beyond humanity? You do as Henry did, and cut it out, put it in your hand, and run back to camp to show your friends. Like the Allagash Four, you tell everyone, because it verifies your experience.

Three of the four still attend UFO conventions, swear that they were probed by ashen beings with almond eyes, but I wonder if it all feels a little like holding wet wood in the morning, like trying to convince the world that the brown chips in your hand once glowed so bright you could see the wrinkles of your palm.

After darkness fully closed on the lake, I looked up often as John and I paddled, nearly praying to see fire in the sky.

Australian fossils show that flies have been around for about 41 million years, which means that flies bothered even the first human.

Blackflies swarmed my neck and back as John and I paddled closer to the island. They bit through my T-shirt, leaving my lower back looking like what Jenny would later describe as "bubbling lasagna." "I now first began to be seriously molested by the black fly," Henry wrote on July 27, the day he arrived on Pillsbury Island. "A very small but perfectly formed fly of that color, about one tenth of an inch long, which I first felt, and then saw, in swarms about me, as I sat by a wider and more than usually doubtful fork in this dark forest path. The hunters tell bloody stories about them,—how they settle in a ring about your neck, before you know it, and are wiped off in great numbers with your blood. But remembering that I had a wash in my knapsack, prepared by a thoughtful hand in Bangor, I made haste to apply it to my face and hands, and was glad to find it effectual, as long as it was fresh, or for twenty minutes, not only against black flies, but all the insects that molested us."

I gripped the giant DEET can and sprayed it across my arms and legs as if I were trying to block in a solid color of spray paint. The repellent replaced the sweet, piney scent that was wafting over the lake. Now I only smelled chemicals. "They would not alight on the part thus defended," Henry wrote after applying his own bug repellent. "It was composed of sweet oil and oil of turpentine, with a little oil of spearmint, and camphor. However, I finally concluded that the remedy was worse than the disease. It was so disagreeable and inconvenient to have your face and hands covered with such a mixture."

John shared Henry's view. He didn't want DEET on his skin, and he didn't get bitten almost at all.

We arrived on the shore of the island under a thin moon. In the dim light, we saw another bullfrog, sitting on a rock near where we hauled up the canoe, bookending our journey, and then never saw another frog for the rest of the trip.

We stood at the campsite, my flashlight illuminating a little brown sign reading, shockingly, *Thoreau*. I'd found Pillsbury Island by tracing his route as written in *The Maine Woods*, comparing it to a map, confirming landforms. I'd been proud to investigate and conclude his northernmost point, and so staring at the sign felt both disappointing and somewhat amazing: John and I had navigated not only to the right island but also to the very site where—at least the National Park Service thought—Henry had camped. It would have saved a lot of time if I'd just looked up the names of campsites in the Allagash.

"Well," I said to John, "Looks like we're here."

We unloaded the bags, then stripped and walked into the lake. John swam far; I stayed closer to the island, only as deep as I could stand, up to my chest, washing the blood from my back and arms and neck, and then realized that I was washing DEET into the lake and so got out, ashamed that the first thing I did to this pristine water was add pollutants and my own blood to it.

The grass within the campsite was the kind I'd seen only in botanical gardens. Soft and papery, as if underwater. Wavy and full-bodied and liquid green.

"I groped about cutting spruce and arbor-vitae twigs for a bed," Henry wrote of sleeping outdoors. "I preferred the arbor-vitae on account of its fragrance, and spread it particularly thick about the shoulders. It is remarkable with what pure satisfaction the traveler in these woods will reach his camping-ground on the eve of a tempestuous night like this, as if he had got to his inn, and, rolling himself in his blanket, stretch himself on his six-feet-by-two bed of dripping fir twigs, with a thin sheet of cotton for roof, snug as a meadow-mouse in its nest."

We slept outside that first night, on the grass. Tired from the long drive and the paddle up the lake, we fell asleep quickly.

I was awoken by loons singing to each other, which sounded as mystical and haunting as the first time I heard them as a boy. "In the middle of the night," Henry wrote the night before he entered Eagle Lake, "as indeed each time that we lay on the shore of a lake, we heard the voice of the loon, loud and distinct, from far over the lake. It is a very wild sound, quite in keeping with the place and the circumstances of the traveler, and very unlike the voice of a bird."

It *is* very unlike the voice of a bird, partly because it is so loud, so echoey, so vast, so, as Henry pointed out, humanlike: "I could lie awake for hours listening to it," he wrote. "It is so thrilling . . . This of the loon—I do not mean its laugh, but its looning,—is a long-drawn call, as it were, sometimes singularly human to my ear."

A small animal shouldn't make a sound so melodious, so operatic, instrumental. Like a flute played in a canyon. The vastness of looning is partly because of the

GRASS AND PINE, THE ISLAND

lake's hard surface rimmed by the wall of trees, like a drumhead. Lakes are different from the sea not just in salt, and not just in dark water or fauna: lakes are bells. "It was unusual for the woods to be so distant from the shore," Henry wrote of this lake, "and there was quite an echo from them . . . I was shouting in order to awake it."

The warm wind pushed against the trees as I lay there in the grass listening to the looning. The loamy scent of fresh water passed over me. The dark was so clear that I couldn't distinguish the constellations I knew within the crowds of new stars. The Milky Way combed the silhouettes of the overhead evergreens.

I had no dreams that night, though I kept telling myself before I fell asleep to remember my dreams.

This 1857 journey was far more menacing than Henry's other two through Maine—not because of what he writes about, but what he doesn't, and what trembles just under the surface of his thirteen days out there.

It started when Henry arrived in Bangor on July 20, 1857. He went to his cousin-in-law, George Thatcher, who was Henry's travel agent for his Maine journeys, so George could set him up with a guide. George introduced Henry to Penobscot guide Joe Polis, who lived outside Bangor. As Henry wrote of the first exchange,

Joe, who'd been scraping a deerskin when Henry and George arrived at his house and didn't pause his work during their conversation, agreed to guide Henry—not because he wanted to show the botanist Maine's flowers, but because, as Henry wrote, "His brother had been into the woods with my relative [George Thatcher] only a year or two before, and the Indian now inquired what the latter had done to him, that he did not come back, for he had not seen nor heard from him since." Joe was going to guide Henry so he could look for his missing brother.

Henry doesn't note if George responded to Joe, whether George knew what had happened to the brother. The wording here, "what the latter had done to him," is disturbing, unavoidably violent.

Throughout the following two weeks in the woods, Henry was unsympathetic to Joe's search, but did sometimes mention it: "The Indian went up to the house to inquire after a brother who had been absent hunting a year or two," he wrote, halfway through their journey. Another time: "Our path ran close by the door of a log hut in a clearing at this end of the carry, which the Indian, who alone entered it, found to be occupied by a Canadian and his family, and that the man had been blind for a year. He seemed peculiarly unfortunate to be taken blind there, where there were so few eyes to see for him. He could not even be led out of that country by a dog, but must be taken down the rapids as passively as a barrel of flour."

Joe never found his brother, and if he received any news of him, Henry didn't note it. I might have thought, in part, that it simply didn't interest Henry, that his bitterness spanned from Concord social-ites to wilderness guides. He was sometimes cruel or cold in his writing about people—like in *Cape Cod*, when walking Provincetown's streets, he was "agree-ably disappointed by discovering the intelligence of rough, and what would be considered unpromising, specimens." But the way he wrote about Joe Polis is different. He called Joe a "wild beast," and mocked the way he spoke English. When Joe sang to Henry and Ed—a tender moment with the three huddled in one small tent, trying to fall asleep under the pattering rain—Henry wrote, "There was, indeed, a beautiful simplicity about [the song]; nothing of the dark and savage, only the mild and infantile." When they pad-dled across a bay and Joe offered the origin story of the mountain in front of them, Henry's response was, "An Indian tells such a story as if he thought it deserved to have a good deal said about it, only he has not got it to say, and so he makes up for the deficiency by a drawling tone, long-windedness, and a dumb wonder which he hopes will be contagious."Another time, describing a conversation with Joe, Henry wrote, "His answer, in such cases, was never the consequence of a positive mental energy, but vague as a puff of smoke, suggesting no *responsibility*, and if you considered it, you would find that you had got nothing out of him. This was instead of the conventional palaver and smartness of the white man, and equally profitable."

To be clear, Henry David Thoreau was a famous abolitionist who, for instance, spoke beside Sojourner Truth at an antislavery rally on the Fourth of July 1854, at which he said, "The inhabitants of Concord caused the bells to be rung and the cannons to be fired, to celebrate their liberty—and the courage and love of liberty of their ancestors who fought at the bridge. As if *those* three millions had fought for the right to be free themselves, but to hold in slavery three million others." He publicly railed against the 1850 Fugitive Slave Act, and helped escaped slaves along the Underground Railroad. He was an outspoken critic of what he called Massachusetts's moral hypocrisy and the "cowardice and want of principle of Northern men" in antebellum America. "Practically speaking," he wrote in *Civil Disobedience*, "the opponents to a reform in Massachusetts are not a hundred thousand politicians at the South, but a hundred thousand merchants and farmers here, who are more interested in commerce and agriculture than they are in humanity." These acts and writings were important and mattered, especially for a public figure. "There are thousands who are *in opinion* opposed to slavery and to the war, who yet in effect do nothing to put an end to them," he wrote. He wanted to put an end to them.

But to not pause on those passages about Joe—and the racial stereotypes therein—would be whitewashing and, more importantly or maybe interestingly, not seeing how racism informs and shackles a person's actions despite their political and cultural beliefs. It wasn't misanthropy—or not only misanthropy—that made Henry so uninterested in Joe's search for his missing brother, which surprised me, because I guess I never thought his heart could be so far from people he professed to love. Or, another way to say it: for a man who hated roads and industry and wanted to live outside his time, he was surprisingly *of* his time here in his descriptions of Joe, of the blandly cruel racism and stereotyping that informed environmental, political, and many levels of social decision-making in the nineteenth century. For a man who was so clear-eyed about justice or analytically poetic about a flower he passed on a morning walk, his sight was constricted. The evidence is also in this fact: like Joe, Henry also lost his brother, but because Henry couldn't penetrate the border between their identities, he couldn't see—or didn't mention—that they shared the same shattering loss. They were together brotherless. Henry seemed the blind man here, whom Joe was leading through the woods and lakes and down the rivers "as passively as a barrel of flour."

This is the land of abductions, I thought when I came upon the UFO story after reading about Joe's missing brother. Of people losing themselves, of taken people.

Maybe I'm just reading distance or disdain within Henry's perspective, but Joe didn't seem to like Henry very much. "In answer to the various observations which I made by way of breaking the ice," Henry wrote of the morning he and Joe met for the journey, "he only grunted vaguely from beneath his canoe once or twice, so that I knew he was there." Still, in their separation, we do get some facts about Joe's life. We know that he was forty-eight when he guided Henry, and that he had a sweet tooth. We know that he was partially deaf in one ear, so always slept on his side, with his good ear up. He was religious, prayed twice a day, and almost died of starvation one early winter when he was a boy, hunting with two older men. He saved them all by catching an otter, eating it, and boiling lily roots with otter oil to make soup. He had a wife, who was at home while he was with Henry, and whom Henry only mentioned when they returned.

Our first morning on Pillsbury, John and I canoed around the island after drinking a few cups of coffee. A creamy blue sky overhead. John caught a fish with big copper-colored scales. He swung the rod over to my side of the canoe, and I unhooked the fish, tossed it back. A river otter raised its head by our canoe twice, then disappeared underwater.

Sometime during that day, far out on the lake, I heard singing. I'd heard it the night before, too, and dismissed it as wind or the pockets of clapping water made by our paddles. Or something mixed with birdsong? But now, here it was again. I put the paddle in my lap and listened, passing my mind over explanations. It was warbling, far off. I could make out syllables, pauses. The clear cadence of sentence to a melody. Then it stopped.

"I hear singing," I said to John, confidently.

"That's so weird," he said. "I did too. Last night?"

"Right now and last night."

I didn't have anything else to say, and neither did John, about the voices we both heard. Perhaps it was people singing across the lake. But why for two days straight? Maybe there was a camp somewhere nearby, and sound does travel farther across water than you think.

We let the singing go on, and then it faded, and then we didn't say anything more about it. That night, I wrote in my journal, *It sounds like humming coming from the sky*. For the rest of that day, I smelled the faint scent of fish wafting from my hands and the floor of the canoe.

There was a third man on Henry's walk—botanist Ed Hoar, who had grown up near Henry and spent his professional life collecting grasses. Ed and Henry were the infamous pair that mistakenly burned down three hundred acres of forest near Concord. They'd lit a campfire to cook fish they'd caught.

Ed was thirty-four, six years younger than Henry, when they went to Maine together. The only way to really be with Henry David Thoreau, Ed wrote in a letter to another friend, was "to go with him in his walk; to walk long and far; to have wet feet, and go so for hours; to pull a boat all day; to come home late at night after many miles. If you would do that with him he would take you with him. If you flunked at anything, he had no more use for you." I'd think that Ed was a weathered outdoorsman, able to keep pace with Henry. But in Maine, he proved otherwise. He was nearsighted, which made the dense forest trouble for him. His wet and blistered feet slowed everyone down. He was often exhausted and dozed off in the canoe, for which Joe scolded him. He forgot things, all the time, like when he left his knife at camp, and they all had to paddle back, against the river's current, to get it. He later forgot his camping gear altogether, and then, heading off alone to retrieve it, got lost. "It was as if he had sunk into the earth," Henry wrote. "This was the more unaccountable to me, because I knew that his feet were, since our swamp walk, very sore, and that he wished to keep with the party . . . I hastened along, hallooing and searching for him, thinking he might be concealed behind a rock." Within hours of being found, Ed got lost, again. So lost this time that he slept alone that night. "The darkness in the woods," Henry wrote of stopping the search for Ed, "was by this [point] so thick that it alone decided the question."

Still, Henry felt tenderly toward his friend: "I thought what I should do the next day if I did not find him, what I *could* do in such a wilderness, and how his relatives would feel, if I should return without him . . . Yet we must try the harder, the less the prospect of success."

Ed spent years trying to keep up with Henry. Collecting, learning from his brilliant friend. Nights sleeping side by side. Days listening to birdsong. Witnessing an icon of American nature writing; humanizing Henry for us. I like seeing Henry through Ed's eyes, like when Ed described how Henry would "get up in dark night and watch for hours the lightening around a rotten log in Maine."

And yet, only after Henry died—five years after they went to Maine together—did Ed have a startling realization: "I have just finished reading Thoreau's *Winter*," Ed wrote in a letter. "I have greatly regretted that I did not know Thoreau better." We can spend hours, days, months, maybe a lifetime with each other, Ed was realizing, without asking the only questions that matter. They had shared botany and ornithology instead of intimacy, and now Henry was gone.

I reread "A Winter Walk," keeping Ed's regret in mind, searching for what might have triggered it, but I lost all concentration on their friendship in the beauty of the writing. It's a simple essay, about waking up early on a New England morning after a snowstorm, when the snow and frost on his windowpanes emitted a "dim and private light" within, and the distant early morning sounds of someone chopping wood or cows lowing were "twilight bustle . . . too solemn and mysterious for earth." You can sense Henry's body here: "The floor creaks under our feet as we move toward the window to look abroad through some clear space over the fields. We see the roofs stand under their snow burden." I can see his warm feet—perhaps in socks—padding across the cold wood floor to peer out at what last night's blizzard had done. By the early evening of his walk, Henry skates down a river that winds through towns and countryside. He skates over flooded meadows, through beds of frozen cranberries mixed with meadow grass.

Ed married his neighbor, Elizabeth, and they moved to Sicily, where they grew citrus trees and figs. They had a daughter. Did Ed, looking out to the hot Sicilian mountains, perhaps cutting into a fig, think of walking with Henry? Of spending that night lost in the Maine woods, scared, wishing he was lying beside Henry on a bed of spruce, listening to Joe sing them to sleep?

We can't stay beside—live with, spend weeks with, confide solely in—our friends forever. We pair off to marriages, move, grow our families. I see John a few times a year now—usually for a few days. When I do see him, I'm sometimes distracted by our first year together, how surprised I was to encounter in him the sudden ease and depth of friendship you might find once, twice in a lifetime. How many of us feel the first encounter of our friend throughout the friendship, an echo in friendship? Or not an echo, because I don't exactly feel a repetition of ten-year-old memories. I'm thinking of something more internal, some earlier identity of mine that presents when I'm around John. When we met, I was twenty-six, and so my life through his eyes starts at twenty-six, with all the uncertainty and vague ambitions that come with being twenty-six. In a way, I will always be twenty-six around him, will always be the person spending an hour after leaving my internship walking around Noe Valley, sniffing for jasmine, wondering if I should apply to graduate school.

When Henry died, Ed lost a witness of himself at a certain age at a certain time. Ed might have lost himself as the wood-smoked, bewildered young man wandering through the forest, might have lost a perspective of himself as the admiring younger man seeing Henry David Thoreau sitting on a log, waiting for dawn. I don't think this is hyperbole, that friends keep and then offer past identities to each other. I feel energetic when I'm around John, sometimes a little childish, hungry to impress, just as I was when we first met. Is this why a parent's death is so devastating? That of all the witnesses lined up in your life, losing a parent is losing the biggest one, the one who drummed you up out of nowhere and saw you, and saw you, and saw you? This is no stranger than a physical truth I read some years ago, that my mother might still be carrying some of my own fetal cells in her bloodstream, carrying something of myself that even I don't have anymore.

A neighbor of mine, Emily, is a neuroscientist with young twin boys. She is a professor at UPenn, but she and her husband, a cryptologist, moved to our town, to live in a little cottage by a salt marsh, when the pandemic washed away their schedules in Philadelphia. In the summer, Jenny and I walked with them through cow fields and along beaches, grateful to hear what these intelligent young parents had to say. When we got to talking about shedding identities as we grow into adulthood, Emily wrote a long email to Jenny about loss:

> Since our cells refresh and turn over so quickly, what makes us who we are isn't the physical

combination of cells in our body, but rather the patterns of how they work together—and certainly within the brain it is the patterns of firing and connection rather than any specific collection of neurons that render our thoughts and feelings and who we are. There is so much reuse and repetition in biology and evolution, it makes sense that some of those same patterns would repeat themselves in other bodies, rather than uniquely starting over each time. So in thinking about new life and loss, I'm also filled with wonder in thinking about the ways that our soul could be encoded in the patterns of firing not only in our own brains, but also in how those patterns get transmitted beyond our individual brains. The patterns our thoughts and feelings and actions set in motion ripple out in their impact, growing, adapting to new environments and challenges in this world. By extension, in this way, I think, to some degree, that souls don't observe strict boundaries of "mine" or "yours," but rather exist in an interconnected set of patterns that carry our essence forward, distributed across people and time. In that way, we get to live many lives. By extension, your you-ness is stored in yourself, and also distributed across the safe places and people you have already touched and interact with.

That's exactly what I feel when I see John now—that he holds something that he isn't aware of holding. That part of myself, which might not feel like my current self, is "distributed" to him. He doesn't hold part of my identity, because I don't feel a deficit in myself when I'm not around him—no, it's something that exists more in the alchemical realm of language, like a word we share and which I never use unless we're together.

A windstorm in the afternoon. I lay down in the grass while John sat by the firepit, staring at a spider. I watched a cluster of dragonflies eddied in the lee of a towering pine. *Their wind tent*, I wrote before napping.

I woke to a grouse skulking around in our camp, clucking in the shadows. The pattern of sticks and shadows and sunlight on its feathers—making itself known only in the foliage it disrupted underfoot and its popping, jolting movements. I asked John if he wanted to go for an evening paddle

We slid the canoe into the lake.

Ten minutes away from the island, John said, "Looks like rain in the north." Some minutes later, he said, "The wind has changed." Still, somehow neither of us anticipated what happened next. The sky went yellow, like the kind I've seen before a tornado, and a warm lip of forerunning wind introduced a storm that came down in streams, and, after passing, left us drenched and seated in front of a sunset as yellow-smeared as one in a Turner painting.

The wind nudged the canoe south, pointing us, nearly unbelievably, toward a double rainbow bent over our island. As if a signature, certifying our luck. "Who does not feel that here is a phenomenon which natural philosophy alone is inadequate to explain?" Henry journaled on an August day in 1852. "The use of the rainbow, who has described it?"

John and I, too, were at a loss for words for these weightless strips of light: we said, only, *Wow*, and *Do you see that?* between our long silences.

"If I were to choose a time for a friend to make a passing visit to this world for the first time," Henry wrote, reflecting on rainbows, "perchance it would be at a moment when the sun was setting with splendor in the west, his light reflected far and wide through the clarified air after a rain, and a brilliant rainbow, as now, o'erarching the eastern sky . . . If a man travelling from world to world were to pass through this world at such a moment, would he not be tempted to take up his abode here?"

Have you noticed that landscape paintings almost never show rainbows? Rainbows are too obvious in their beauty, and paint is an insufficient material to show something made of nothing but light. That all white light is collapsed colors is easy to forget: a rainbow has the character of an arriving stranger, not the remarkable and slivered performance of our common daylight. They probably stopped even early humans in their tracks.

The sunset to our west now appeared less like a sunset and more like saffron clouds slowly erupting from the mountain range.

We stashed our paddles and floated.

We talked about John's dad, who had passed away when he was a boy.

The wind had died, and so the sky was reflected clearly on the becalmed water. I felt suspended, lifted to the sky, as if our canoe were floating. Our hair was still wet from the rain.

I asked about his own pending fatherhood. He said something poetic and truthful, which I wish I had transcribed, but didn't because it seemed an intrusion. Reflecting here, I think I understand something more of why Henry journaled, and why there is so much good writing in it, so little lazy writing, so many elaborate metaphors and full sentences. Writing is willing permanence. If I remembered what John had said about becoming a father, I would return to it here, I would feel the sensation of his words here again, and so make it permanent. I would not live it again—the sound of John's voice under the gloaming sky, the satisfaction of arriving in deep territory after days of lighter talk—but I would be able to replicate and hold some of the sensation. I could refill myself with that sensation, as you might hold a water glass under a tap. Writing is the glass, I see.

We paddled back to the island, and fell asleep in our tents because the rain had returned.

The next morning, our last morning on the lake, I heard a man's voice carried across the water.

"I want ten grand," he said.

I was sipping coffee John had made.

I walked to the shoreline, curious to see who had so clearly stated his cash goal.

The young man was sitting at the front of a canoe, shirtless, his long hair spilling over his shoulders.

Another guy, at the stern, was more clothed, but both were wearing identical floppy camouflage-patterned sun hats. They looked like they were in college, or just out.

They paddled by our island, but didn't see me sitting on the shore.

"I've never had ten grand," the one in front continued—nearly yelling, jacked, I assumed, on the big blue morning, the early start they must have gotten, their sliding canoe, the wind pushing them from behind, the sun on their faces. He was happy. He had ripped his shirt off. He was screaming about money.

"I have a good job," he continued. "It pays more than any job I've had. But still I think I could do better. Yeah. Ten grand! I'd be all set with ten grand."

I was in a place so distant, by some standards, that the paved roads had ended, cell service gone, that otters swam up to your canoe and frogs let you stand toe-to-face. And still, I thought, we all bring in our worries, our regular hopes. What we want from a job. Whom we miss. Henry wrote in "Walking," "I am alarmed when it happens that I have walked a mile into the woods bodily, without getting there in spirit. In my afternoon walk I would fain forget all my morning occupations and my obligations to society. But it sometimes happens that I cannot easily shake off the village. The thought of some work will run in my head, and I am not where my body is,—I am out of my senses. In my walks I would fain return to my senses. What business have I in the woods, if I am thinking of something out of the woods?" In our campsite had been a printed sign pinned to a post, warning of coronavirus. Indeed, we couldn't easily shake off the village.

I wondered what the guy would do with the ten grand, and why he'd been so reasonable, here in the wilderness, when he could yell for a hundred grand or a million. By the time they'd paddled away, I admired him. He would likely get that ten grand sometime in his life. He had taken time off from work to paddle with his friend, and one of them must have bought the matching hats for their trip. He was in control of what he wanted, and was getting it.

"Ready to go soon?" John said at my back.

I walked to our campsite.

I shook the rain fly off my tent, laid it on the grass to dry. I saw then that my tent—shelled of the fly— was not assembled correctly, the way it was slumped to the left and cratered in the crown. I looked at John, to see if he noticed. He was busy stuffing the last items into his backpack.

I stared back at my tent, wondering where to start, when I saw movement beyond the campground, at the edge of the dark forest. Something darted in the shadows. Something bigger than a squirrel. It was close—maybe twenty, thirty feet away.

"Did you see that?" I said to John.

"What?"

"In the woods," I said.

I walked around my tent, toward the trees.

From behind a pine, something like an inflated weasel leaped into view, and then hopped closer to camp, slowly and playfully, in a motion that might be described as a weightless Slinky.

"There!" I said to John.

The animal disappeared behind another tree.

John came to my side.

We stared into the columns of tree trunks still blackened by last night's rain.

The animal then sprang into a clearing. It stood on its back legs to show its pale chest.

"That's not a weasel," I said. This was bigger, and had a sweet, puppyish face.

"What do you think?" John asked.

I'd never seen one, and still don't know how I knew the name except for the fact that Henry mentioned them a few times in his journals, but the term came to me clearly.

"Pine marten," I said.

It had either been habituated to people or was naively unaccustomed, because it came close enough for me to see its black eyes, pinkish ears, and whorls of ivory fur mixing with the darker fur.

Suddenly, it turned and ran away, much faster than it had approached, scared by something we'd done or the way we'd moved. Or, likely, the marten's curiosity had been shattered by the sudden clarity of our human bodies' outlines and smells, which, for most animals, are things only to fear—things that bring with them abstract thought, lethal cunning, and weaponry that have peeled our species away from the animal kingdom as a whittler's blade curls up a shaving.

"First time I've seen that," I said.

I turned back to my tent, thinking I might have permanently damaged the poles by the way I'd bent them to fit into the wrong clips.

We paddled home, down the lake, in the direction of the two young men.

White birch trees look like capillaries against the dark evergreens, I noted when I paused paddling.

THE DAY WE LEFT

The wood thrush, the other great singer on these lakes, called from the forest. Its voice, as disembodied as wind through rigging, is so much richer than birdsong. "And sitting in that dusky wilderness," Henry wrote, "under that dark mountain, by the bright river which was full of reflected light, still I heard the wood thrush sing, as if no higher civilization could be attained."

We walked the canoe back up the stream, passing no frogs. We loaded it onto John's truck, and drove back without getting lost.

Jenny and Rebecca met us at the door in the early evening. Jenny screamed when I lifted my T-shirt and she saw my bug-bitten back. I showered, and then we all went to a hilltop restaurant where the tables were outside and far apart. The owner had planted a wall of flowers that was weeded and tidy. We were all trying to do our best in the pandemic.

After dinner, in bed, I picked up an annotated selection of Henry's journal, and turned to the index to find a passage on frogs. I was still thinking of the bullfrog on the stone, and wondered if Henry had any thoughts. There was a lot on frogs. *Frogs: bull frog. Frogs: dreaming. Frogs: hyla. Frogs: pickerel. Frogs: wood.*

But just above *Frogs* was *Friendship*. Though I was tempted to see what *Frogs: dreaming* was, I picked a page on *Friendship*, considering the trip I'd just taken with John, wondering if Henry might be able to articulate what I couldn't. He could:

> I sometimes awake in the night and think of friendship and its possibilities, a new life and revelation to me, which perhaps I had not experienced for many months . . . I wake up in the night to these higher levels of life, as to a day that begins to dawn, as if my intervening life had been a long night . . . I rise into a diviner atmosphere, in which simply to exist and breathe is a triumph, and my thoughts inevitably tend toward the grand and infinite, as aeronauts report that there is ever an upper current hereabouts which sets toward the ocean . . . Friendship is the fruit which the year should bear; it lends its fragrance to the flowers, and it is in vain if we get only a large crop of apples without it.

I've thought of these last lines often since I read them—friendship, companionship, closeness, and apple blossoms. That we can eat and sleep and work and make

APPLE BLOSSOMS, FRIENDSHIP

our own happiness in our houses without friendship, but what we feel missing without it is like the flowery tips of an apple tree in spring.

Before I turned off the bedside light, I flipped to *Frogs: dreaming*. There, I found a passage that had led to my original search for Henry's thoughts on bullfrogs: "The sound of the *dreaming* frogs prevails over the others," he wrote about the nighttime. "Occasionally a bullfrog near me made an obscene noise, a sound like an eructation, near me. I think they must be embodied eructations. They suggest flatulency."

So, *dreaming frogs* were his words for singing frogs, likely wood frogs; and bullfrogs are not holy guardians of rivers and lakes—rather, living burps.

Months passed, summer passed. I hadn't thought about the Allagash until the autumn air came, when the heating in our house started failing and I called my neighbor, who has his own HVAC business.

He looked at the heating unit, and then we got talking about the summer. He'd been hiking, canoeing. I told him about canoeing on the Allagash, and he said he had a cabin there.

"Where?" I asked. "In the Allagash?"

"Yeah," he said. "Near Eagle Lake."

"Eagle Lake," I said. "That's right where I was. For this Thoreau thing."

"Pillsbury Island?" he said. He knew of the Thoreau campsite.

We'd been up there at the same time, in June—he was only a couple of miles away from the island, in his cabin.

"Strange," I said. Whenever there's a coincidence like this, I try to pay attention.

I asked him about the alien abduction, if he'd heard of it.

"Oh yeah," he said. "It's famous up there."

"Did you ever see anything?" I said, smiling.

"No," he said. "But I've seen something else."

He took out his measuring tape for no apparent reason.

"I was sitting by Churchill Lake with my dad, drinking a beer, in the afternoon. We'd just come back from a seven-day canoe trip. Rained every day. Raining that morning, too. We were leaving. And it was clearing up, just then. The clouds moving away. Clouds like *The Simpsons* clouds, you know?"

I said yes.

"Like puffy? Like drifting across with patches of blue?"

"I know exactly what you mean," I said.

"So" he said. "I look up, and there is a hole in the sky."

"A what?" I said.

He then held up his measuring tape at arm's length, as if he was screwing in a lightbulb.

"A hole. The size of this measuring tape, but up in the sky. The clouds would move towards it, and then separate around it. It was a perfect circle of blue when a cloud passed through it. So. You know what that is."

I likely whispered the question, "What?"

He clipped his measuring tape back on his belt.

"Wormhole. That's why the aliens came. They use wormholes to travel between galaxies, and there just happens to be one above the Allagash."

"A wormhole?" I said.

"You probably think I'm crazy. But that's what I saw. My dad saw it too. A blue circle in the sky. Physics can prove that shit. You don't have to believe me. Doesn't matter."

I thought of Joe's brother; of the hole in the sky; of a loon turning into a fireball that fell from the sky; of a glowing cloud carrying a person; of passageways to places from where you can't return; of John's crossing into fatherhood. *If a man travelling from world to world were to pass through this world at such a moment,* I felt with John on the lake, *would he not be tempted to take up his abode here?* What is this persistent human belief in otherworldly wandering, this distant before-life and after-life catching our eye when our own world reveals itself at its most beautiful?

"You want fan heating, or radiant?" he asked, leaving me with more questions than he could answer.

Interlude IV

Walking in the mountains one winter, some years ago, I came upon a lamb without eyes. Ravens lifted and settled on a nearby oak, folding themselves in the wind. That's how ravens kill lambs, I was told—by taking out the soft parts first, the lips and the tongue, too, if they can get it. The lamb was on its side, and a snowdrift had filled the small harbor of its belly. Of the whole walk that afternoon, in the mountains and sheep pastures, I remember only generally the sky and winter-stripped trees, the stone walls and the fact that I'd gotten lost. But with photographic clarity I can see the lamb—the terrible hollows in its head, the way the snow gathered on its wool—as if it were a statue I'd come a long way to see.

"Why is it that in the lives of men we hear more of the dark wood than of the sunny pasture?" Henry wrote in his journal a few years before he died. Why is it, I agree, that the darker moments of life more easily stick with us, are retold more often? I'm suspicious of scientific explanations that say fear or grief teaches us something, that the dark stains on one's memories are a constellation of lessons for survival. Like, if you were chased by a saber-toothed tiger, you'd tell your friends about it, with all the fear you felt, and they would avoid the tiger, live to tell others, and so create a chain-link of narrative to protect everyone from tigers. Those who told stories of bad things that happened to them survived. Those who listened, survived, and the warnings continued as facts of good inheritance. But it seems to me less likely that fear or grief could help us live—in fact, just the opposite: that a bit of forgetfulness would teach us more fully, if the purpose of teaching is to thrive. Forgetting the dark woods of our lives might help us *survive* our own lives more easily. The traumas in a life that can wither your sense of self and purpose don't seem very biological, anatomical. Losing a brother, as Henry David Thoreau did, is not the same as touching a flame and remembering by the burn not to touch it again. No, I don't think the darkness of the woods is a teaching tool—more, it is the spirituality of a life, and that is why we hear about the dark woods more often. A forest is a rich ecosystem with animals that were alive before humans, with mushrooms that were alive before animals; a pasture is food for cattle. There is more divinity in the dark woods.

I remember the lamb so clearly, I think, because of its suffering. A newborn lamb dying for its eyes, to give a bird some hours of energy, has no answer, no explanation, and so my mind must stall on it and memorize it, try to enter the meaning as if it were a locked house whose every door and window I rattled. The lamb's life seems too big a sacrifice, and I realize that sad stories often come from imbalanced sacrifices. The dark woods, small or large—a lamb's death, a brother's death, a family's inherited anger—force us to examine questions above our anatomy, above common reason, and that's why we like to retell them, I think, to be reminded of questions without answers, questions that might be described only within a sense of spirituality. In other words, walking through the dark forest, you might eventually look up through the trees, see that the sky above is the same as the sky over the sunny pasture, that it is one canopy of light spread over your whole life's landscape. Grief and joy are in the same life, but it's only in the forest where you notice the shafts of sunlight spilling through.

That first summer I followed Henry's journeys, I sometimes went for walks in the middle of the night. Short ones—down the driveway, or to the water's edge. One August night, standing by the salt marsh, I saw, in the grass flooded by the tide, a blinking yellow-green light. Bioluminescence: the sparking plankton that comes every late summer to coastal New England. The plankton light up when touched, when roiled in waves, when stirred with a paddle or by dock pilings. This one, caught in the drowned grass, was shaking alight with the liveliness of an autumn leaf rattling on a branch. It entranced me, this neon marble inserted in the subdued tones of night. It also seemed wrong to me, that this small, vivid performance more likely would have gone unnoticed, without announcement, had I not walked down there at that moment. What is that feeling, to meet nature with a witness, the same one that I had when John and I pointed out the rainbow to each other? It's odd to think that nature requires company, because, of course, it doesn't.

THE DARK WOOD

Cape Cod, Again

I didn't walk to Provincetown this time, because I wanted to go with Jenny, follow the same path along the outer beaches. But she couldn't walk with me—not twenty miles in the sand, not ten miles in the sand. Jenny is pregnant.

I wrote my friend Mary—the one whom I met in Provincetown years earlier, the one who invited me back for lox and showed me her and her wife's pot garden. Mary told me that she had a connection to the dune shacks, those cabins on the outer wrist of the Cape where, she said, Annie Dillard had written. She said if we wanted, Jenny and I could just drive to Provincetown and stay in a shack, write a different sort of story. She reserved us two nights in early September.

229

Unlike last time going to Cape Cod, there was no rush to leave, no nightmare driving me from home. Jenny and I drank coffee in bed, with our dog, Sally, lying across our legs as she likes to do. I pointed out the window, at geese flying up the river, and wondered where the summer had gone. We talked about the news, about how we should stop talking about the news. John and Rebecca had just visited with their six-week-old baby, John Emmanuel, and we talked

about how John Emmanuel seemed to have changed just in their short visit—he'd come to our house with roaming eyes, but on the day they left, he was looking at us, staring.

We spent an hour putting together snacks and dinners for the two nights, assembling a tote bag that had sausages and cheeses and oat milk in a jar. We dropped Sally off at our neighbor Cheryl's house, then picked tomatoes and cucumbers from her garden after she insisted there were too many for her to eat. We stopped at the general store. We bought a straw basket, plus a couple more groceries.

"This is not like my last trip to the Cape," I said to Jenny as we drove away from the store. "I am shopping with my fiancée."

"Isn't it so nice?" she said.

We crossed the Bourne Bridge splitting a clementine, then drove down old Route 6, the more meandering variation of the highway striping Cape Cod. The whole car smelled of citrus.

It was a sunny day. The sky rich blue. The sun on the trees and stone walls was a different light, a distinctly early autumn light that reminded me of soccer practice and the first days of school—sunlight that might be described as cold or lemony, but it is anything but cold, because it is a homecoming light, a light at the end of summer, which was better described by Henry in 1852: "There is a silvery light on the washed willows this morning, and the shadows under the wood-sides appear deeper, perchance by contrast, in the brilliant air. Is not the air a little more bracing than it was? . . . The sky is more beautiful, a clearer blue, methinks, than for some time past, with light and downy clouds sailing all round a quarter of the way up it . . . From the shore I hear only the creak of crickets. The winds of autumn begin to blow."

"It really is so nice," I said to Jenny. "Last time I did this, I was walking barefoot on a beach with blisters on my feet and a block of cheese in my backpack."

We stopped to visit Randy and Pat, my hosts years ago in Wellfleet, who had a second home in Barnstable.

Randy had just self-published the book he was writing when I first met them. He was proud of the reviews that had been posted online. He wanted to give me a copy.

The four of us sat in chairs on their lawn, masked and distant. We talked about his book, about how his son helped him with the cover art. Pat said the rosebushes that I'd planted at their house in Wellfleet were thriving.

I asked if their lives had changed much, out here on the Cape, with the pandemic. "I'd think things would pretty much stay the same."

"Oh," Pat said. "Well, we can't do our challenge-level square dancing now."

"Challenge square dancing?" I said.

Randy appeared a hardened New Englander, a man who'd chop you a cord of wood in a day and not necessarily into upper-level dancing.

"We had to leave the Cape to do it," Pat said. "To Boston. Marlborough. Out of state. When you do it at the level we do it at, you have to travel."

Pat wanted to show us the house before we left. Near the dining room were antique paintings of her relatives. A husband and wife—stiff-necked, waxy-skinned, and deprived of painting techniques that

233

would come to America generations later and lift portraiture out of doll-faced renderings.

The man's head tipped forward, like he was about to nod off. The woman looked frightened, the way her eyes bulged. Her eyelids were rash red.

Randy pointed to the man.

"That one looks drunk."

He then pointed to the woman.

"And that one looks like she can't get over her wedding night."

"Randy," Pat said, smiling, tapping his arm.

With Randy's book in hand, Jenny and I bid them farewell.

"That was a pleasant stop," Jenny said.

"Just a very pleasant stop," I said.

Crossing into the next town, we pulled into another general store, where Jenny bought cookie cutters, and I picked out a bone-white ceramic water pitcher.

"Are you hungry?" I asked, seeing a seafood restaurant on the side of the road.

We were going to be very late to Provincetown. On this same trip, years ago, I had walked to Wellfleet and found a bed in a stranger's home long before we'd even drive past Wellfleet today.

"Lobster rolls?" Jenny said, as I pulled into the restaurant's parking lot.

We walked up to what looked like an ice-cream window—with an unreadably long menu tacked beside it. After some discussion about why someone would ever want lemon on a lobster roll instead of mayonnaise, we ordered two mayonnaise lobster rolls. The young woman behind the window took our order, head down, writing.

"I'm freaking out right now," she said, calmly, as if she were asking if we wanted a side of pickles, still writing out the order. "I love you," she said to Jenny.

Sometimes, when this happens, I think how startling it could be if I weren't expecting it. But people act all sorts of strange ways when they recognize Jenny. Some are abrasive—coming up to her with their phone outstretched and wanting a selfie. Some are kind— introducing themselves and saying how much they admire her work. Some are vulnerable—looking in her eyes and describing their feelings. Some quietly point, or take pictures secretly. Some, like when we're crossing a street in New York, scream out her name. The first summer Jenny and I were dating, John and I were on another canoe trip, paddling down a river in Maine. Somewhere along the way, out of the blue, John asked me how Jenny's celebrity affected me. Nobody had asked me that, I realized then, and it was not something I had ever expected to encounter in my life. "Having strangers randomly come up to the person you love and say they love her, too," I said, "is really nice."

"Oh," Jenny said to the woman taking our lobster roll order. "What's your name?"

They had a short conversation, and then the woman said we could take a seat outside, and she'd bring out our order.

I bought a Sierra Mist, and Jenny made fun of me, and I said that Sierra Mist is a perfectly adult drink, tons of adults drink it. We sat down on sun-warmed benches, the sweet smell of early fall and fried food wafting over our table, sharing my Sierra Mist, eating our overstuffed lobster rolls and french fries. I texted Mary, said we were going to be even later. We were fluttering down the Cape, the day as expansive and limitless as the autumn sky.

"Mind if we make one more quick stop?" I asked Jenny when I recognized the sandy driveway that I'd taken years earlier—the entrance to the number-less forked roads that would bewilder me through a turkey-filled forest and lead me to the alewife pond.

"I'm in no rush," she said

I pulled up a satellite map, recognized—not so far ahead of us—the lawn where I'd stood years earlier. The oysterman's house. Instead of rowing through lily pads as I had with Randy, I arrived by way of the driveway this time. I parked just out of view of the house.

"This might be awkward," I said to Jenny when I turned off the car.

When I was alone, I didn't mind if I looked stupid or worked awkwardly through an explanation of why I was standing on someone's doorstep. But with her there, I felt a small weight of expectation, the accountability of a witness.

She said she didn't mind.

We walked, holding hands, on either side of a grass strip curving through the forest, dead-ending at the oysterman's house. Bordering the front lawn of the house was a picket fence swathed by petal-thinned rudbeckias foreshadowing fall.

"Think someone's home?" Jenny asked.

Near the front door was a beach towel, laid out to dry. A nearby umbrella stand was open. A hanging pot of geraniums looked well-watered.

"Must be," I said. "I don't know what I'm going to say. Just—maybe they'll give us a tour of the house?"

I stepped onto a timeworn brick path, which led to a front door. I knocked. Nobody answered. I knocked again, called hopefully, "Hello?"

Maybe they were napping. Showering. Out on the pond.

I looked back. Jenny stood in the driveway, resting her hands on her belly, staring up into the trees. The sun was in the last third of the sky. Light swept through the overhead pine trees, cupping every small growth with a private shadow and invigorating the lawn and pine needles and flowers to near fluorescence. Jenny's yellow skirt, rounding over her stomach, glowed.

"Nobody home?" she said.

"I don't think so," I said. "Oh, well. We're late, anyway."

I didn't want to feel the awkwardness of standing on someone's door, just then.

"Let's go," I said.

"Want a picture of the house?" she asked. She stood in front of the fence, looking toward the front door.

"Sure," I said.

We met Mary behind the gate that led to the dunes. She and her wife, Marian, a Guggenheim Fellow and

THE OYSTERMAN'S HOUSE, AGAIN
(WHERE HENRY SLEPT)

renowned photographer, had become Jenny's and my good friends. They'd been to our house. They'd met both Jenny's and my parents. I had given Marian an exhibition at the art gallery where I curate shows. They were, Jenny and I said, our fairy godmothers.

"You look the same," Mary said to Jenny, "except you've got a basketball!" She pointed to Jenny's belly. "Oh my gosh you look so so so good!"

The shacks are hidden far from the road, embedded behind enormous dunes and only accessible by four-wheel drive on hazardous and hilly sand-roads. We loaded our tote bags and baskets of snacks into Mary's Jeep, and then she drove us away, into the dunes. As she recounted the history of the shacks—preserved in the 1980s for artists and writers to use—her whole body bounced on the driver's seat, her two hands gripping the wheel seemingly the only thing keeping her head from bonking the car roof.

We arrived at the shack. Mary gave us a tour, especially excited about the wooden outhouse that looked out over beach roses and west, to the sunset. "Just go with the door open," she said. "You can't beat that view."

Inside, the shack reminded me of an old ship's below-decks. It was twenty feet long and seventeen feet wide, made of weatherworn, silvered wood. A half dozen lanterns were arranged by a table by an old stove. Fishing lures hung from the walls, and oars repurposed as hangers crisscrossed the ceiling. Field guide books, tucked away in all the corners, named the local mammals, amphibians, birds and plants and stars seen from Cape Cod. Dunes swelled on three sides of the shack, as if they were about to swamp it. Atop the dunes were sand-stunted beach plums and beach roses whose flowers I could smell through the wide, screened windows. Water came from a hand pump on the southern side of the shack, which—if the lanterns and smell of old wood didn't do it—eased me into thoughts of another century. I haven't been in a house recently with so few plastics. The silverware was kept in old tin cans.

Mary said goodbye, that she would come back with Marian in two days, and not to worry, there was really good cell service. We could call if we needed anything. She left.

Wind blew through the screened windows, making a *si-sh* sound—that of hundreds of wires cutting air.

The sun was setting.

The crickets started.

I lit three lanterns, and the wood inside glowed orange.

OUTHOUSE, DUNES, PROVINCETOWN

Jenny and I began making dinner. I put on the kettle to boil water for rice. Jenny cut a cucumber we'd picked from the vegetable patch that morning. I cut sausages, then tipped the cutting board over a skillet that she had heated. She brought out cheese and crackers. Sometime during the cooking, Jenny took over stirring, and I had mixed the boiling water and rice and tossed in a pat of butter, and then I made her a cheese-and-cracker. I put the forks and knives out. She found napkins. We ate under the lambent lantern light, to the blended sound of crickets and ocean and wind.

Later that night, I wrote in my notebook while Jenny read *Suite Française* beside me. Two lanterns burned on the bedside tables. I had trouble seeing what I was writing because the pen's shadow crossed the ink—both black lines followed the pen's nub, and both lines contrasted harshly on the paper. It was disorienting, and made me wonder about all the shadows people had dealt with before overhead lights. Not only the black triangular shadow of a pen's nub but also those of forks on a dinner plate, or hands on a face, or a warped book page fanning a shadow across text. The many black strikes crisscrossing a dining room lit by lanterns may have been normal once, until electricity washed them away—not so much like the sun, but a soaking rain that touches everything.

I didn't like writing much by hand, anyway, because my handwriting is not my own now, since I'm left-handed and my fingertip was shortened. It is painful, too, even years after that winter. The grafted skin has no spectrum of touch: it is either numb or has a buzzing sunburnt feeling. I can't control a pen like I used to, and I'm sad to lose my handwriting, and know that it will likely never come back.

After ten minutes of writing, my eyes hurt from strain, and I closed the notebook.

I wondered if the crickets would ever quiet down, and fell asleep thinking of that.

I woke up in fog, smelling roses.

What did Jenny and I do all day? I can hardly remember now, and found even less urgency to take any notes.

I remember sitting in a yellow rocking chair, looking at the dune grass quiver, and overhearing Jenny listen to a self-hypnosis program called the Gentle Birth Method. I've heard it many mornings, so know many of the lines—like the one about the uterus being shaped like a hot-air balloon, how the cervix is the basket; or how you must ask your baby to tilt her head when she's ready to move through the birth canal so that her chin touches her chest; or of the euphoria you'll feel when she lies on your chest.

I looked through a book of Delacroix's drawings that Mary had left for me.

In the late afternoon, I told Jenny I was going to the beach for a walk, to see if I could gather any of the feelings of the windblown solitude I'd felt a couple of years earlier. I didn't want to feel alone, self-loathing, and bitter, as I had before, but I did want to see purpose in the landscape, the way the landscape had felt therapeutic. Was being troubled a requirement of seeing meaning? If I felt content, was there something that seeped away from the clouds and dune grass? When I had walked in the forest at the foot of Wachusett Mountain, I looked at mushrooms and envied them, their brainless growth, their clear purpose, their vacuum of human troubles. They had one job, and they did it with colorful purpose. I don't envy a mushroom now. I didn't want to be in crisis. Still, I wanted the revelation that came at the end of my first Cape walk: that following Henry led to hidden, unexpected goodness.

I stopped walking less than a quarter mile from the dune shack, sat in the sand, watched three gray seals forage in the surf, and only thought how I wished Jenny was there so I could point out the seals and we could watch them forage together.

Henry didn't have a partner or lover that I know of—man or woman. He had friends, people he went on walks with, but even the closest among them—the clumsy and bewildered Ed Hoar—admitted he didn't know Henry very personally. He admired people, like Ralph Waldo Emerson, but was he intimate with anyone? In writing about sex in nature—in the shape of mushrooms or flowers—he offered little of his own sexuality, aside from reprimand and remorse: "I lose my respect for the man who can make the mystery of sex the subject of a coarse jest, yet, when you speak earnestly and seriously on the subject, is silent." Or: "Whatever may befall me, I trust that I may never lose my respect for purity in others. The subject of sex is one on which I do not wish to meet a man at all unless I *can* meet him on the most inspiring ground." Or, this oddity: "I would preserve purity in act and thought, as I would cherish the memory of my mother." Still, did he want to be with someone? A neighbor? A friend? Reading through his journals, I often wondered whose body, whose sexuality, did he want to drive away from his thoughts? Whose image did he try to outpace with long walks or writing or by hemming himself into a shack by a pond? Or, more tempting to wonder, was one of those people alongside him, all the while?

Gray seals have sorrowful dog eyes, I wrote in my notebook, before standing, startling the seals, who dove underwater frightened, leaving three smooth disks where their bodies had sunk. I headed back, toward Jenny.

The smell of tomato sauce filled the shack.

"Dinner is all ready," Jenny said, when she saw me at the doorway. "You want the sauce on top of your spaghetti, or should I just mix it all in?"

I looked at my pregnant fiancée lit by early evening sun. The pasta's steam rose into the light too, looked to be lapping up the light.

I didn't want to walk anymore. I didn't want to sleep in a stranger's house. I didn't want to wake up before dawn to hike up Mount Katahdin or take MDMA under a chairlift or empty my breath and be pressed by the weight of Walden Pond. I didn't want to think about a porcupine's heart, or why dreams count, or have any revelations at all. I only wanted to have dinner with Jenny, tell her about the seals I'd seen, ask her what she thought they might have been foraging, and then light a few lanterns and read in bed beside her before we both fell asleep.

"Sauce in, or on top?" she said again, her back turned to me.

"Whatever you want," I said.

"On top, then," she said. "You like that."

Just then, there seemed nothing more interesting in the landscape—no seal or wind-tussled dune grass or spume or volcanically red sunset—than having a conversation with my fiancée. Talking with her was bigger than what I might find in a forest, stranger than bioluminescent wood: to speak with someone I loved. To, in other words, translate the electricity in my head to my lips and tongue and throat, and to listen to her do the same. And by that, make these two lightless, enclosed spaces of our bodies find each other.

I took a seat at the table that Jenny had already set.

We woke just after dawn to more fog, which seemed to gather sound closer to the ear. I heard Jenny turn on the stove's gas, click the lighter—the rush of a small flame spread under the kettle. The fog had welled on the window screens, and fell in droplets when I touched them.

We drank coffee in bed, talked about how bad our dreams had been, and how strange that was considering the landscape around us, with its sincere and subdued beauty. I once described sleep as the "necessary dark territory we enter alone"—without thinking about how irrelevant that is the moment you wake up with someone you love beside you.

The fog burned off the sea by midmorning, and everything around the cabin changed as it hardened into sight. The beach plums, roses, grasses.

"But this shore will never be more attractive than it is now," Henry wrote, of autumn in Provincetown. "Such beaches as are fashionable are here made and unmade in a day, I may almost say, by the sea shifting its sands."

We finished our coffee, started to clean up the cabin before Mary returned to take us back. I walked outside to the pump, filled a bucket with water, and then poured it in a cistern connected to a pipe running to the kitchen sink. I stood on a bench, empty water bucket in my hand, and looked down to the sand, where I saw what looked like small animal prints stitching long lines all around the cabin.

So we'd been visited in the night, when I thought we were alone.

Home, Again: *The Axle of the Universe*

And now, I am home, writing in my dad's old painting studio, which has the same turpentine and wood smell I remember as a boy. Jenny is up at the house, working on her second book, by a fire I built for us this morning. It is October. A north wind has been blowing for two days, as it does every early October, and has scrubbed the sky of all clouds. Over the past week, fallen leaves have found their ways into the footings of the house and stone walls. Beside me are three editions of Henry David Thoreau's journals, and I'm tempted to thumb to his October entries, to scan for the words *Autumn* or *Fall* or *Leaves* or *Foliage*, to read how he would describe leaves gathered by the wind. But this must end somewhere.

I can't stop looking at the salt marsh, stretching out just below the window of the studio. I've been told that the salt marsh is a fragile habitat. That it takes thousands of years to make the right spongy mud, seed the right grasses. But in my thirty-plus years of looking out at this same half acre of marshland, it seems anything but fragile. It is a lawn that ends as cleanly at the edge of the forest as it does on the ocean side, barring all other plants. It resists everything but itself. An untended, unbreachable swath of grass, alive with crabholes and ready for two high tides a day and thickly green. I've seen three hurricanes overwhelm it, and then recede. I mean, what seems fragile, what is known as rare, is far stronger—drowned then parched, drowned then parched. The in-between space. Once, a therapist told me that it's strange that people want to get through grief quickly, because grief is the in-between time, a period of fragility that brings your emotions closest to the surface. All stories are about passages, she said.

Six months after Henry's brother died, he went for a walk. West, to Wachusett. "We will remember within what walls we lie," he wrote about that walk, "and understand that this level life too has its summit, and why from the mountain-top the deepest valleys have a tinge of blue; that there is elevation in every hour, as no part of the earth is so low that the heavens may not be seen from, and we have only to stand on the summit of our hour to command an uninterrupted horizon."

On the last autumn night Jenny and I were in Massachusetts, before we moved back to LA for the winter so she could birth our daughter and recover there, I walked out to the marsh. I carried a bowl of dinner leftovers and old cheeses and vegetables we'd cleaned out from the fridge, to dump in the sea. Sally had snuck out of the house and stood beside me, on the dock, sniffing at the bowl. The tide was receding, the water draining loudly in rivulets through the grasses. Overhead and beyond the edge of the marsh: stars and reflections of stars. I dumped the food, then put the bowl down for Sally to lick. I looked for the Swan in the stars, but couldn't find it. I listened to Sally's tongue on the bowl, to the bowl ringing on the wooden boards, to the draining marsh.

There was a time when I was afraid of the night, when my subconscious would loosen and scare me awake. Now I loved the night, the way I felt pocketed in home, the sky husked of blue to show ancient pins of light. I would never want to bypass those sleepless nights and anxiety because of this fact: that the stars had not changed, the river had not changed, the marsh had not changed. As in, the world around me was always there and waiting to be seen again when I was ready, and when I was ready, it looked only beautiful. Nature does not need revelations of itself to be itself. A swirl of bioluminescence in the river on a late August night will not wait for me.

Even standing in the low grass, elevation.

I picked up the bowl, and headed home.

LIGHT IN THE GRASS

There, in that Well Meadow Field, perhaps, I feel in my element again, as when a fish is put back into the water . . . All things go smoothly as the axle of the universe.

—Henry David Thoreau, thirty-nine years old
(January 7, 1857)

Endnotes

CAPE COD

page 3: ". . . there is elevation in every hour, as no part of the earth is so low that the heavens may not be seen from, and we have only to stand on the summit of our hour to command an uninterrupted horizon." Henry David Thoreau, "A Walk to Wachusett," in *The Writings of Henry David Thoreau*, edited by Bradford Torrey (Boston: Houghton Mifflin, 1906), 150. First published in January 1843, in the *Boston Miscellany*.

page 8: "The sea-shore is a sort of neutral ground, a most advantageous point from which to contemplate this world." Henry David Thoreau, *Cape Cod* (Boston: Houghton Mifflin, 1914), 224. Originally published posthumously by Ticknor and Fields, 1865.

page 9: "junk of heavy cake" Robert Packard, "Walking Cape Cod With Thoreau," *New York Times*, July 8, 1979, https://www.nytimes.com/1979/07/08/archives/walking-cape-cod-with-thoreau-walking-cape-cod-with-thoreau-if-you.html

page 10: ". . . a vast morgue, where famished dogs may range in packs, and crows come daily to glean the pittance which the tide leaves them." Thoreau, *Cape Cod*, 224.

page 15: "I am all broken down this year." Thoreau, *Cape Cod*, 95.

page 22: "I love any other piece of nature, almost, better." Henry David Thoreau, *The Journal: 1837–1861*, edited by Damion Searls (New York: New York Review Books, 2009), 22. February 21, 1842.

page 23: ". . . fire-boards as well as the casements rattle well that night." Thoreau, *Cape Cod*, 114.

page 25: For further reading on climate change in relation to blooming times, see: Richard B. Primack, *Walden Warming: Climate Change Comes to Thoreau's Woods* (Chicago: The University of Chicago Press, 2014).

page 27: "At length, as we plodded along the dusty roads, our thoughts became as dusty as they; all thought indeed stopped, thinking broke down, or proceeded only passively in a sort of rhythmical cadence of the confused material of thought." Thoreau, "A Walk to Wachusett," 150.

page 36: "Why was there never a poem on the cricket?" Thoreau, *The Journal: 1837–1861*, 73. September 3, 1851.

MOUNT KATAHDIN

page 51: "I stand in awe of my body." Henry David Thoreau, *The Maine Woods* (Boston: Houghton Mifflin, 1906), 78. Originally published by Ticknor and Fields, 1864.

page 51: "*Contact! Contact! Who* are we? *where* are we?" Thoreau, *The Maine Woods*, 79.

pages 56–57: ". . . laying the twig end of the cedar upward, we advanced to the head, a course at a time, thus successively covering the stub-ends, and producing a soft and level bed." Thoreau, *The Maine Woods*, 60.

page 57: ". . . these bright fluviatile flowers, seen of Indians only, made beautiful, the Lord only knows why, to swim there!" Thoreau, *The Maine Woods*, 59.

page 57: "condensed cloud" Thoreau, *The Maine Woods*, 69.

page 58: "This night we had a dish of arbor-vitae or cedar tea, which the lumberer sometimes uses when other herbs fail . . ." Thoreau, *The Maine Woods*, 60.

page 58: "In the night I dreamed of trout-fishing . . ." Thoreau, *The Maine Woods*, 61.

page 62: "Shouldst thou freeze or starve, or shudder thy life away, here is no shrine, nor altar, nor any access to my ear." Thoreau, *The Maine Woods*, 70–71.

pages 62–63: "The tops of mountains are among the unfinished parts of the globe . . . a slight insult to the gods to climb and pry into their secrets, and try their effect on our humanity." Thoreau, *The Maine Woods*, 71.

page 67: "I must receive my life as passively as the willow leaf that flutters over the brook." Henry David Thoreau, *The Writings of Henry David Thoreau, Journal I: 1837–1846*, edited by Bradford Torrey (Boston: Houghton Mifflin, 1906), 326. March 11, 1842.

page 67: "Now the wind would blow me out a yard of clear sunlight, wherein I stood . . ." Thoreau, *The Maine Woods*, 70.

page 68: "I most fully realized that this was primeval, untamed, and forever untamable *Nature*, or whatever else men call it, while coming down this part of the mountain." Thoreau, *The Maine Woods*, 77.

WACHUSETT MOUNTAIN

pages 79–80: "If you have an inclination to travel, take the ether; you go beyond the furthest star." Henry David Thoreau, *The Writings of Henry David Thoreau, Journal II: 1850–September 1851*, edited by Bradford Torrey (Boston: Houghton Mifflin, 1906), 194. May 12, 1851.

page 81: "Earth laughs in flowers." Ralph Waldo Emerson, "Hamatreya," *Selected Poems 1876* (James R. Osgood and Company, 1876). Originally published in 1847.

page 81: ". . . the murmuring of water, and the slumberous breathing of crickets, throughout the night." Thoreau, "A Walk to Wachusett," 141.

page 81: "When we reached [the summit] we felt a sense of remoteness, as if we had traveled into distant regions, to Arabia Petræa, or the farthest East." Thoreau, "A Walk to Wachusett," 142–43.

page 82: "So solemn and solitary, and removed from all contagion with the plain." Thoreau, "A Walk to Wachusett," 144.

page 82: "My body was the organ and channel of melody, as a flute is of the music that is breathed through it." Thoreau, *The Journal: 1837–1861*, 90. October 26, 1851.

page 85: "How ample and roomy is nature." Thoreau, "A Walk to Wachusett," 146.

pages 86–87: "These bristly fellows are a very suitable small fruit of such unkempt wildernesses." Thoreau, *The Maine Woods*, 242.

page 91: ". . . so rich and lavish is that nature which can afford this superfluity of light." Thoreau, "A Walk to Wachusett," 145–46.

HOME

pages 95–96: "He is treading his old lessons still, and though he may be very weary and travel-worn, it is yet sincere experience." Thoreau, "A Walk to Wachusett," 150–51.

page 99: "My waking experience always has been and is such an alternate Rough and Smooth." Thoreau, *The Journal: 1837–1861*, 431. January 7, 1857.

PART TWO

page 113: "At this distance it is more ideal, like the landscape seen with the head inverted, or reflections in water." Thoreau, *The Journal: 1837–1861*, 258. April 20, 1854.

SOUTHWEST

page 115: "The future lies that way to me, and the earth seems more unexhausted and richer on that side." Henry David Thoreau, "Walking," *Atlantic Monthly*, June 1862, 662.

page 120: For Annie Dillard's insights on the origins of sand, see: Annie Dillard, *For the Time Being* (New York: Alfred A. Knopf, 1999).

page 123: "Bring your sills up to the very edge of the swamp." Thoreau, "Walking," 666.

page 123: "Two or three hours' walking will carry me to as strange a country as I expect ever to see." Thoreau, "Walking," 660.

page 149: "The first step to a remedy is that the people care. If they know, they will care." Henry Demarest Lloyd, *Wealth Against Commonwealth* (New York: Harper and Brothers, 1894), 535.

page 150: "To help them to know and care; to stimulate new hatred of evil, new love of the good, new sympathy for the victims of power, and, by enlarging its science, to quicken the old into a new conscience, this compilation of fact has been made." Lloyd, *Wealth Against Commonwealth*, 535.

page 150: "Democracy is not a lie." Lloyd, *Wealth Against Commonwealth*, 536.

page 151: ". . . prepared to send back our embalmed hearts only as relics to our desolate kingdoms." Thoreau, "Walking," 657–58.

page 152: "I think that I cannot preserve my health and spirits, unless I spend four hours a day at least—and it is commonly more than that—sauntering through the woods and over the hills and fields, absolutely free from all worldly engagements." Thoreau, "Walking," 658.

page 153: ". . . and sometimes, no doubt, we find it difficult to choose our direction, because it does not yet exist distinctly in our idea." Thoreau, "Walking," 661–62.

INTERLUDE III

pages 160–61: "The surface of the snow in the fields is that of pretty large waves on a sea over which a summer breeze is sweeping." Thoreau, *The Journal: 1837–1861*, 107. January 22, 1852.

page 161: "Is not January the hardest month to get through?" Thoreau, *The Journal: 1837–1861*, 250. February 2, 1854.

page 162: "My soul and body have tottered along together of late, tripping and hindering one another." Thoreau, *The Journal: 1837–1861*, 22. February 21, 1842.

pages 162–63: "I was walking at five, and found it stinging cold. It stung the face." Thoreau, *The Journal: 1837–1861*, 310. February 6, 1855.

page 163: "This, i.e. yesterday, the 6th, will be remembered as the cold Tuesday." Thoreau, *The Journal: 1837–1861*, 310. February 7, 1855.

page 164: "What else can we sing, and our voices be in harmony with the season?" Thoreau, *The Journal: 1837–1861*, 249–50. January 30, 1854.

THE ALLAGASH

pages 167–68: "Our doubts are so musical that they persuade themselves." Thoreau, *The Journal: 1837–1861*, 23. March 11, 1842.

page 171: "Their light is singularly bright and glowing to proceed from a living creature." Henry David Thoreau, *The Writings of Henry David Thoreau, Journal IV: May 1, 1852–February 27, 1853*, edited by Bradford Torrey (Boston: Houghton Mifflin, 1906), 145. June 25, 1852.

page 173: *Allagash* means "hemlock bark." Thoreau, *The Maine Woods*, 254.

page 174: ". . . live and die and never hear of the United States." Thoreau, *The Maine Woods*, 260–61.

pages 174–76: "It could hardly have thrilled me more if it had taken the form of letters, or of the human face." Thoreau, *The Maine Woods*, 198–200.

page 177: "It was impossible for us to discern [the] trail in the elastic moss, which, like a thick carpet, covered every rock and fallen tree, as well as the earth." Thoreau, *The Maine Woods*, 236.

page 178: "The coasting down this inclined mirror, which was now and then gently winding, down a mountain, indeed, between two evergreen forests, edged with lofty dead white pines, sometimes slanted half-way over the stream, and destined soon to bridge it." Thoreau, *The Maine Woods*, 278.

page 180: "We heard an ox sneeze in its wild pasture across the river." Thoreau, *The Maine Woods*, 317.

pages 181–82: Personal accounts from abductees: *The Joan Rivers Show*, as uploaded here: https://www.youtube.com /watch?v=DGPF4--Fq9E

page 182: For more on the experiences with aliens recounted by the four friends who visited the Allagash, see: Matt Byrne, "Unafraid of Alienating Themselves," *Portland Press Herald*, September 7, 2013.

page 182: "Yeah, we were definitely stoned when we went out on the lake just before we got that sighting." Jessica Potila, "Subject of 1976 UFO Incident Casts Doubt on 'Allagash Abductions,'" *Fiddlehead Focus*, September 10, 2016.

page 183: "Nature must have made a thousand revelations to them which are still secrets to us." Thoreau, *The Maine Woods*, 200.

page 184: ". . . then it turned itself into a great ball of fire, and fell swiftly down to the water; and when it struck the water, the earth shook and the roar of it was great." Joseph Nicolar, *The Life and Traditions of the Red Man* (Bangor, ME: C. H. Glass, 1893), 105.

pages 184–85: "And the clouds turned white and the brightness of fire was not there." Nicolar, *The Life and Traditions of the Red Man*, 10.

pages 185–86: ". . . and for a few moments I enjoyed fellowship with them." Thoreau, *The Maine Woods*, 200–201.

page 187: "I kept those little chips and wet them again the next night, but they emitted no light." Thoreau, *The Maine Woods*, 201.

pages 188–89: ". . . not only against black flies, but all the insects that molested us." Thoreau, *The Maine Woods*, 236–37.

page 189: "It was so disagreeable and inconvenient to have your face and hands covered with such a mixture." Thoreau, *The Maine Woods*, 237.

pages 190–91: ". . . rolling himself in his blanket, stretch himself on his six-feet-by-two bed of dripping fir twigs, with a thin sheet of cotton for roof, snug as a meadow-mouse in its nest." Thoreau, *The Maine Woods*, 265.

page 191: "It is a very wild sound, quite in keeping with the place and the circumstances of the traveler, and very unlike the voice of a bird." Thoreau, *The Maine Woods*, 247.

pages 191–93: "This of the loon—I do not mean its laugh, but its looning,—is a long-drawn call, as it were, sometimes singularly human to my ear." Thoreau, *The Maine Woods*, 247–48.

page 193: "It was unusual for the woods to be so distant from the shore, and there was quite an echo from them . . . I was shouting in order to awake it." Thoreau, *The Maine Woods*, 230.

page 194: ". . . and the Indian now inquired what the latter had done to him, that he did not come back, for he had not seen nor heard from him since." Thoreau, *The Maine Woods*, 175.

page 194: "The Indian went up to the house to inquire after a brother who had been absent hunting a year or two." Thoreau, *The Maine Woods*, 265.

pages 194–95: "He could not even be led out of that country by a dog, but must be taken down the rapids as passively as a barrel of flour." Thoreau, *The Maine Woods*, 234.

page 195: ". . . agreeably disappointed by discovering the intelligence of rough, and what would be considered unpromising, specimens." Thoreau, *Cape Cod*, 261.

page 195: "wild beast" Thoreau, *The Maine Woods*, 180.

pages 195–96: "There was, indeed, a beautiful simplicity about [the song]; nothing of the dark and savage, only the mild and infantile." Thoreau, *The Maine Woods*, 198.

page 195: ". . . so he makes up for the deficiency by a drawling tone, long-windedness, and a dumb wonder which he hopes will be contagious." Thoreau, *The Maine Woods*, 191.

page 196: "This was instead of the conventional palaver and smartness of the white man, and equally profitable." Thoreau, *The Maine Woods*, 180.

pages 196–97: "As if *those* three millions had fought for the right to be free themselves, but to hold in slavery three million others." Henry David Thoreau, "Slavery in Massachusetts," in *The Essays of Henry D. Thoreau*, edited by Lewis Hyde (Albany, CA: North Point Press, 2002), 184.

page 196: ". . . a hundred thousand merchants and farmers here, who are more interested in commerce and agriculture than they are in humanity." Henry David Thoreau, "Civil Disobedience," in *The Writings of Henry David Thoreau*, 362. First published in 1849.

page 197: "There are thousands who are *in opinion* opposed to slavery and to the war, who yet in effect do nothing to put an end to them." Thoreau, "Civil Disobedience," 362.

pages 198–99: "In answer to the various observations which I made by way of breaking the ice, he only grunted vaguely from beneath his canoe once or twice, so that I knew he was there." Thoreau, *The Maine Woods*, 176.

page 199: For more on Joe Polis, including further reading in Notes, see: Thomas Lynch, "The 'Domestic Air' of Wilderness: Henry Thoreau and Joe Polis in the Maine Woods," *Weber Studies* 14.3 (Fall 1997): 38–48.

page 200: "If you flunked at anything he had no more use for you." Edward Hoar to Edward S. Burgess, December 30, 1892, in *Thoreau in His Own Time: A Biographical Chronicle of His Life, Drawn from Recollections, Interviews, and Memoirs by Family, Friends, and Associates*, edited by Sandra Harbert Petrulionis (Iowa City: University of Iowa Press, 2012).

page 201: "The darkness in the woods was by this [point] so thick that it alone decided the question." Thoreau, *The Maine Woods*, 285–87.

pages 201–202: "Yet we must try the harder, the less the prospect of success." Thoreau, *The Maine Woods*, 286.

page 202: ". . . get up in dark night and watch for hours the lightening around a rotten log in Maine." Edward Hoar to Edward S. Burgess, December 30, 1892, in *Thoreau in His Own Time*, 142.

pages 202–3: "I have greatly regretted that I did not know Thoreau better." [note: italics added to "Winter" earlier in quotation] Edward Hoar to Edward S. Burgess, December 30, 1892, in *Thoreau in His Own Time*, 141.

page 203: "dim and private light" Henry David Thoreau, "A Winter Walk," in *Henry David Thoreau: Collected Essays and Poems*, edited by Elizabeth Hall Witherell (New York: Library of America, 2001), 92. Originally published in *The Dial*, 1843.

page 203: ". . . twilight bustle . . . too solemn and mysterious for earth." Thoreau, "A Winter Walk," 93.

page 203: "The floor creaks under our feet as we move toward the window to look abroad through some clear space over the fields. We see the roofs stand under their snow burden." Thoreau, "A Winter Walk," 92.

page 208: "The use of the rainbow, who has described it?" Thoreau, *The Writings of Henry David Thoreau, Journal IV: May 1, 1852–February 27, 1853*, 288. August 7, 1852.

page 208: "If a man travelling from world to world were to pass through this world at such a moment, would he not be tempted to take up his abode here?" Thoreau, *The Writings of Henry David Thoreau, Journal IV: May 1, 1852–February 27, 1853*, 287–88. August 7, 1852.

pages 211–12: "What business have I in the woods, if I am thinking of something out of the woods?" Thoreau, "Walking," 659–60.

page 216: "And sitting in that dusky wilderness, under that dark mountain, by the bright river which was full of reflected light, still I heard the wood thrush sing, as if no higher civilization could be attained." Thoreau, *The Maine Woods*, 302–3.

page 217: "Friendship is the fruit which the year should bear; it lends its fragrance to the flowers, and it is in vain if we get only a large crop of apples without it." Henry David Thoreau, *I to Myself: An Annotated Selection from the Journal of Henry D. Thoreau*, edited by Jeffrey S. Cramer (New Haven, CT: Yale University Press, 2007), 326–27. July 13, 1857.

page 219: "They suggest flatulency." Thoreau, *I to Myself*, 70. June 13, 1851.

INTERLUDE IV

page 223: "Why is it that in the lives of men we hear more of the dark wood than of the sunny pasture?" Thoreau, *The Journal: 1837–1861*, 473. October 29, 1857.

CAPE COD, AGAIN

page 232: "The winds of autumn begin to blow." Thoreau, *The Writings of Henry David Thoreau, Journal IV: May 1, 1852–February 27, 1853*, 326–27. August 31, 1852.

page 246: "I lose my respect for the man who can make the mystery of sex the subject of a coarse jest, yet, when you speak earnestly and seriously on the subject, is silent." Thoreau, *I to Myself*, 138. April 12, 1852.

page 246: "The subject of sex is one on which I do not wish to meet a man at all unless I *can* meet him on the most inspiring ground." Thoreau, *I to Myself*, 138. April 12, 1852.

pages 246–47: "I would preserve purity in act and thought, as I would cherish the memory of my mother." Thoreau, *I to Myself*, 138. April 12, 1852.

page 249: "Such beaches as are fashionable are here made and unmade in a day, I may almost say, by the sea shifting its sands." Thoreau, *Cape Cod*, 330–31.

HOME, AGAIN

pages 252–53: ". . . there is elevation in every hour, as no part of the earth is so low that the heavens may not be seen from, and we have only to stand on the summit of our hour to command an uninterrupted horizon." Thoreau, "A Walk to Wachusett," 151.

page 257: "All things go smoothly as the axle of the universe." Thoreau, *The Journal: 1837–1861*, 431. January 7, 1857.

Acknowledgments

Thank you, first, to Jennifer Acker and *The Common*, for giving a home to "Three Walks," which would become *Six Walks*. Thank you, Nadja Spiegelman and The Paris Review Daily, for publishing an earlier version of Interlude III. Thank you, Craig Popelars and everyone at Tin House—this has been nothing but the most enjoyable experience. My deepest gratitude goes to my editor, Elizabeth DeMeo, who guided this book through the wilderness with profound kindness and clarity. Claudia Ballard: thank you for your wise counsel and foundational support. Thank you, Jim Tierney, for conjuring up the most beautiful cover, and John Borowicz for spending a day in the marshes with me. Damion Searls: thank you for editing the book that would start my journey. And thank you, my dear parents and brother, for your creativity, curiosity, and imaginations that made our home.

Thanks to those I met along the path: to Pat and Randy for your hospitality and for rowing me across the pond; to

Mary and Marian for opening your home and hearts. John Knight: our friendship has often felt something like drifting on a glassy pond in the far north, saffron clouds overhead. Thank you for our conversations, and for showing up— over and over again. Am I allowed to thank Henry David Thoreau? Well: your brief time on this earth, and how you saw it all and wrote it all down, has made the most profound impact on my deepest core. Thank you for showing so many of us a way to walk through the world.

Thank you, sweet and brilliant Jenny. In some way, I'll always be listening to the ocean and smelling the beach roses at the end of the world with you. This book is for you.

PHOTO © JOHN BOROWICZ

BEN SHATTUCK, a graduate of the Iowa Writers' Workshop, is a recipient of the PEN/Robert J. Dau Short Story Prize and a 2019 Pushcart Prize. He lives with his wife and daughter on the coast of Massachusetts, where he owns and operates a general store built in 1793. His paintings can be found at www.benshattuck.com.